ISBN: 9798321652558

Game, Set, Love

Unless it's Murder

John R Williams

Prologue

$\mathcal{L}$ooking out over the valley below, the view from Point Mountain was not only beautiful, but peaceful and soothing. During their high school days, and after Fred was able to buy his first truck, he and Alice had spent many afternoons and evenings enjoying this vista and each other's company. Although Fred's preteen years were difficult, as high school sweethearts, their lives had been both idyllic and unspoiled. Throughout grade school and high school, they had led simple lives on two farms near Valley Head, WV, but little did they know what twists and turns would lie ahead.

The winding, one-lane dirt road leading to the top of the mountain was narrow and bumpy; some would not call it a one-lane road, since it was really two tire tracks, containing potholes and rocks. Between the tire tracks, the weeds grew without fear of being crushed by heavy tires. On this particular night, the slow 15-minute drive on this 3-mile dirt road was particularly creepy. A slight drizzle permeated the cold mountain air, and Alice was strangely fearful. It was a pitch-black evening and the moon and stars had long been hidden behind the moisture and haze of the mountain. Even though Alice had taken this drive with her boyfriend many times at night, she was always uneasy that something would happen to Fred's old truck and they would become stranded, alone in the dark. The top of the mountain did offer wondrous views in the daytime and at night was a favorite parking spot for teens in Randolph County, WV. But something about this night was different and Alice had a premonition that something harrowing was about to happen.

Chapter 1

After the death of his father in a logging accident, nine-year-old Fred was expected to be the man in the family and do a man's share of the work. Fred's father, Edgar had been driving a logging truck on a downhill stretch of icy road leading into Webster Springs. After an out-of-control slide on the narrow two lane road, he had rolled his truck down the side of the mountain, plunging roughly 100 feet toward the valley below. Because of bad weather, it was three days before rescue workers got to the wreckage. The police report stated that Edgar had died instantly. Fred's mother and her children were traumatized upon hearing of the accident. As the oldest son, Fred had always been a hard worker, but this tragic development in his young life gave him added responsibilities, often pushing his slight frame to exhaustion. At the age of nine, he was given responsibilities about the farm that included babysitting his brothers and sisters, picking fruit in the family's modest orchard, feeding the chickens and gathering their eggs. Fred's mom, Ivy was a capable teacher and experienced in best practices for egg gathering and raising chickens. She taught Fred the lessons that she had been taught by her mother and grandmother.

"Freddie, you need to collect eggs twice a day; mornin and evenin."
"Yes, ma'am."
"And durin winter freezes, three times a day."
"Yes, ma'am."
"Be sure to keep their nest clean with some paddin so the eggs won't break."
"Yes, ma'am, I will."

Fred had been taught from an early age to be respectful towards adults and that included his mother and father. Yes ma'am and yes sir had become second nature and set a nice example for his six younger brothers and sisters. Ivy also instructed Fred on the importance of work, and the daily care of their small flock of chickens provided an integral part of the family diet and Fred's work ethic. Ivy even showed young Freddie how to wring a chicken's neck.

"You just grabbit by the neck and swing it round like so."

This was part of the job that Fred didn't enjoy, but he did enjoy his mom's fried chicken. Fred had names for all 10 chickens and their two-year-old rooster, Ben. Brooding hens would have one or two litters of chicks each year and with a daily harvest of eggs, plus a good source of young chickens, Fred, his mom and six siblings had plenty of eggs and meat for their protein needs. Ivy did all her cooking on a wood-burning pot-bellied stove and she was a wonderful cook. But cooking required a constant need for firewood, and keeping the firewood rack replenished became one of Fred's many chores. Ivy and her seven children lived in a small two-bedroom log cabin with one indoor bathroom and an outhouse. Fred and his three brothers slept in one bedroom and Ivy and the three girls slept in the other. Living conditions were cramped and sharing the indoor bathroom was difficult, but Ivy had a gift for organizing the children and resolving conflicts. By age 12, and after doing the family chores, he was earning money by doing more difficult chores for their closest neighbor; things like baling hay; slopping the pigs and doing minor excavations using the neighbor's tractor.

Three years after the untimely death of his father, Ivy met a man at the Point Mountain Baptist Church, where Ivy and her brood regularly attended church and bible study every Sunday. Leo was a widower and a well-paid supervisor at Mill Creek's only coal mine. After his mom's eventual marriage to Leo, the financial stress on Fred was lessened and he was able to save some of the money he earned from working odd jobs on nearby farms.

At age 14, he saw an old Ford-150 truck for sale while grocery shopping at Valley Head's only food store. It was a two-mile walk from his family's farm to Phil's General Store and Fred was often tasked to do some last-minute grocery shopping. But on this day it was this red truck with a for sale sign on the windshield that captured his attention. Most trucks in the mountain towns of Randolph County were either white or gray, and Fred had never seen a red truck, but this truck drew his attention. For Fred, it was the perfect truck. Because of their low demand, truck dealers in the area seldom had red trucks on their lot. In addition, the resale value of used red trucks was significantly lower, since the farmers of the area mostly wanted colors other than red. This truck appeared to be in mint condition, with new tires and a rust-free paint job. Fred was hoping the truck was also in good mechanical condition. The truck was parked alongside an auto repair shop that was owned by twin brothers, Charley and Harley, but don't let the names fool you. They might sound like a comedy team, but nothing about them was funny. They were two big 24-year-old bullies, who were as mean as they were ugly and were often looking to cause trouble. The boys' father had abused both boys when they were younger and their scarred faces showed the results. Their father mysteriously disappeared soon after the twins' 13th birthday and the father hadn't been seen since. Considering their well-known reputation around town as bullies, Fred warily entered the shop to inquire about the truck.

Chapter 2

$\mathcal{U}$pon entering the shop, Fred saw one brother struggling to repair a truck tire and the other on his back underneath a white Chevy truck.

"I wanted to ask bout the truck for sale."
The brother working with the tire responded, "What you want, kid?"

"How much you want for the truck?"
"Truck ain't for sale."
"But the sign says...
"I said, it ain't for sale and a runt like you ain't got no money to buy it."
"I can pay $500."
"The truck sells for "$1,000."
"Maybe a deposit?"
"Beat it, kid, before I kick yo little ass outta here."

Fred was now a short, stocky kid, and not easily intimidated. He took great pride in being able to stand up for himself. He had been taunted and threatened his entire life by older, bigger kids, and seldom backed down. He had taken some schoolyard beatings, but as he got older, most bullies were reluctant to mess with him. In the two years after his mom's marriage to Leo, Fred had saved $500 selling eggs and doing odd jobs for neighbors. He had continued to do some family chores, but Leo and his brothers were gradually assuming Fred's role as family provider.

"But what if…"
"No, yo scrawny punk, $1000 and notta penny less."

Dejected, Fred turned to leave when he noticed a help wanted sign on the store window. So he decided to ask one more time with a different approach. This time he offered to work for the remaining $500. It was late February and school was still in session. Fred figured that if he worked on weekends, maybe he could earn enough money in six months to buy the truck by summer.

"I saw the 'help wanted' and…"
"No, we want no midget workin here"
"Waita minute," said Charley. "Maybe he could help round here."
Harley responded with, "What work could this little s*** do?"
"We need floors swept, trucks washed and toilets cleaned", Charley said. "If he worked 9 ta 5 on weekends, we could each take a day off on weekends. The kid could even answer the phone and stock shelves."
Harley liked the idea of taking a day off each week.

Charley, whom seemed to be in charge and the brighter of the two, looked at Fred and said, "Sonny, I reckin we can pay $10 a day on weekends for 8 hours of work; two days' work would be $20 per weekend."

"I'll take it," Fred quickly replied. He figured he could save enough to buy the truck by summers' end and it was more than he could make selling eggs and working odd jobs for neighbors. He might even learn something about truck repair. Inquiring about the truck's mechanical condition, Fred asked, "Is the truck in good working order?
Charley replied, "I reckin it is."
"Do ya promise not to sell the truck ta someone else?"
"Sure, kid," replied Charley

Fred knew that the chances of someone offering $1000 cash for an old red truck was slim, since the mountain people of West Virginia seldom wanted red trucks. But Charley's promise was music to Fred's ears and that night, he dreamed of owning and driving his own truck. The next Saturday Fred arrived promptly at 9 a.m. carrying his metal lunch box his stepfather had given him for his 13th birthday. It contained two sandwiches and two slices of Ivy's home-made elderberry pie. Fred had asked his mom to pack an extra slice, figuring he might offer it to whomever was working Saturday. Charley was already there and promptly outlined Fred's chores for the day.

"Sweep the floor, clean the toilet and there's a truck out back that needs washin."

"Yes sir," replied Fred and off he went to clean the bathroom. By noon, Fred had finished the truck washing, the floor sweeping and the bathroom cleaning. He had discovered that beneath the mud and dirt of that truck out back, was a brand new black 1985 Dodge Ram150 beauty. Fred found out later it belonged to the twins. When Charley instructed Fred to take his 15-minute lunch break, he was more than ready for some nourishment. As Fred was eating lunch, he noticed the unkempt appearance of the shop. Tools were scattered everywhere. The auto and truck parts were mixed and disorganized. Fred figured that the twins should be making good money in their small repair shop, but their small run-down farmhouse on the edge of Valley Head told a different story. The twins' mom, unable to take the regular beatings from her husband, had abandoned them when they were five years old. After their father's mysterious disappearance, Charley and Harley had lived alone in the now dilapidated old farmhouse by themselves for the last 11 years.

While eating his lunch, Fred noted that the normally upbeat Charley appeared tired and displeased about something. Hoping to maybe cheer Charley up, he asked, "Would you like a slice of my mom's elderberry pie?"
Charley seemed surprised at this generosity and in his crusty voice replied, "I reckin I would."

As Charley began devouring his pie, his demeanor began to slowly change and he said, "You got more pie?"
"You can have my piece," Fred replied. "I'm really not that hungry."
Fred could have easily consumed the second piece, but thought this might be his best chance to get on the good side of Charley; if there was a good side.

As Fred's first day on the job progressed, Charley gave him additional chores and the first time the phone rang, Fred answered with a cheerful, "Auto Repair Shop, Fred speakin. May I help you?"
Charley was blown away with Fred's phone manners, but also with the way he addressed customers entering the shop. Charley had never been around someone with Fred's manners and Charley noticed.
"Do ya always answer tha phone like that?"
"That's tha way my mom taught me."

Charley seemed to enjoy having Fred around. Fred would soon discover that Charley was better company than his brother.

The next day was cold and snowy and Fred arrived a little late (five minutes to be exact) and Harley was fuming.
"Where ya been kid?"
"Sorry I'm late, tha snow made the walk more difficult than normal."
"That ain't no excuse. I outta dock yo pay."
"I'm sorry, sir."
"Tha toilet needs a better cleanin and tha truck out back needs rewashin and detailed inside an out."

Harley's drive into work had muddied up the truck and on this day a good washing and detailing would take Fred some time. It was cold and windy outside and even though Fred had a warm jacket, the rest of him was cold. The inside of the truck was trashed, with empty beer cans, newspapers and fast food bags and other assorted trash. By lunch time, Fred had finished washing the outside of the truck and went inside the shop to get warm.

"Ya finished?"
"No, sir, I have a bit more ta do."
"Well, git back out there and git her done."

Because it was below freezing and the wind chill was -20°F, Fred was happy to spend the next two hours removing trash and detailing the inside of the truck. A trash bin close by made the trash removal easier. At 3 p.m., Fred had finally finished and headed inside.
"Ya finished?"
"Yes, sir."
"Ok, I reckin ya got 15 minutes ta eat."

As a shivering Fred sat down with cold fingers to eat his sandwich, he warily observed an agitated Harley hard at work on a used Cadillac. Fred knew Harley could be erratic even during the best of times and this was not the best of times. Fred had an extra piece of his mom's pie, but thought that this was not the right moment to offer Harley a slice. So Fred ate his sandwiches and both pieces of pie in silence. Fred spent the rest of the day answering the phone, cleaning the bathroom and sweeping the floor in the customer waiting area. At 5 p.m., Harley was ready to leave. The weather had taken a turn for the worse; blizzard-like conditions; windy and heavy snow.

"Do you mind giving me a ride home?" asked Fred
"Not today, kid, I got places ta be."
"Can you wait until I get my lunchbox?"
"Go ahead, but make it quick."

While Fred was inside collecting his lunchbox, Harley was in the truck admiring the inside. It was as if the truck was brand new. When Fred returned with the shop key, Harley suddenly had a change of heart.
"Git in kid, but don't git no dirt on the seat."
Nothing was said on the ride home and Fred was happy to warm up.

Next Saturday, Fred showed up promptly at 9 a.m. The snow had cleared and it was a bright sunny day. It was a chilly morning, but Fred had dressed more warmly than the weekend before. He figured he might have to spend most of the day outside, so he was better prepared. On this day however, and to his surprise, Charley wanted him to stay inside and answer the phone and organize and clean the brother's tools. In the afternoon, he was to clean the bathroom and finish stocking the shelves.

Chapter 3

$\mathcal{F}$our months passed quickly and Fred had gradually been given more responsibilities. He was put in charge of the customer waiting area and initiated a display area for tires, a table offering free coffee and some additional chairs. Customers seemed happy with the changes and business was brisk. Fred answered all phone calls on weekends and with the aid of the computer, scheduled service appointments and maintained a list of customer contact information. The repair shop was a 60' x 80' steel building with a column-free interior with no separating wall between the customer waiting area and the two bays.

On this clear sunny Sunday morning in late May, Fred was sitting behind the counter in the customer waiting area facing the entrance door. The bathroom was to his left and Harley had just entered to relieve himself when a stranger suddenly barged through the shop entrance. The stranger was a tattooed muscular man over six feet tall, with a pock-marked face and a cruel scowl. After looking around and satisfying himself that Fred was the only one there, he approached the counter.

"May I help you?" inquired Fred.
"You got money in that register?"
"No, sir," replied Fred nervously.
"I don't believe ya, kid."

Having a swastika tattooed on his forehead, a diamond stud in one ear and a handgun in the waistband of his faded jeans, Fred sensed this guy was clearly dangerous. The stranger slowly approached Fred, leaned over the counter, pulled out his gun and pointed it at Fred's nose. He then bellowed in a loud threatening voice:

"Open tha register kid or I'll blow yo face off."

At that moment, Harley exited the bathroom to see what the commotion was all about.

"What tha hell, yelled Harley.

As the stranger turned to his right, he wildly fired a single shot in the direction of six-foot four inch Harley. Fred immediately grabbed his metal lunch box and swung it toward the left side of the stranger's head, knocking him to the ground. Fred and Harley then leaped into action and were on top of the gunman like 'two dogs on a bone'.

Fred grabbed the gun and Harley proceeded to bloody the stranger's face with some vicious blows delivered with fists and elbows. After Harley had thoroughly beaten and subdued the gunman, Fred fetched some rope and they tied up the still unconscious and bloodied stranger. Although Sunday was a tough time to fetch a lawman in the Valley Head area, a call to the sheriff in Mill Creek was successful and soon the gunman was off to jail.

Later that morning, Fred and Harley learned that the clerk in the general store next door had been pistol-whipped and killed by the stranger and roughly $200 was taken from the store's cash register. The gunman had then decided to visit the auto repair shop in hopes of finding more money. At the time of the attempted robbery, the twins had about $2,000 in cash from Saturday's receipts. The morning's episode had earned Fred some well-deserved respect from Harley and at lunchtime, an extra slice of elderberry pie was offered and accepted. They both enjoyed every bite.

During the following week, news of the murder, attempted robbery and the take-down of the suspect by Fred and Harley spread quickly among the families of Randolph County. Local newspapers carried the story as did local TV channels. After seeing themselves on TV doing multiple interviews, Fred and Harley felt like big celebrities.

Next Saturday morning, Fred was greeted at the shop entrance by Charley and Harley with an offer that Fred could not refuse. Charley began by thanking Fred for his bravery and quick thinking, which probably saved his brother's life. Knowing that school would soon be out in early June, the brothers had decided to offer Fred a full-time job for the summer with the official title of office manager.

"We would like to offer ya a full-time job durin the summer; $150 a week for 40 hours of work."
Fred was speechless. He knew the minimum wage in WV was about $120 per week and $150 seemed like a lot of money for a 14-year old. He also figured that he should be able to buy the truck by the time he was 15.
"That would be great! When can I start?"

"How bout June 10th? We can give ya a weekly schedule tomorrow."

"Great, and thank you for the offer," said Fred

During his lunch break, Fred was so excited, he could barely eat. All he could think of was owning and driving his red truck. There was however some unfinished business ahead for Fred and Harley. The trial of the stranger was scheduled for early August and Fred and Harley, being the only witnesses, would need to testify.

Meanwhile, the next four weeks passed quickly and by mid-July, Fred finally had enough money to buy his truck. Fred didn't have a driver's license, but had been driving farm equipment since he was 13. On that day, 15-year-old Fred made the two-mile trip home in his shiny red 1975 Ford F-150 XLT Lariat truck. Charley and Harley watched as Fred turned right onto US Highway 219 and headed south toward Mingo and the family farm. Fred had washed, waxed and detailed his truck inside and out and was beaming with pride as he made the right turn onto the dirt road leading to the family farm. Crossing over the Tygart River on a narrow and rickety wooden bridge, he headed toward the dirt parking area by the barn. He was greeted by his entire family, who oohed and aahed over his shiny red truck. It was by far, the best day of Fred's life.

After multiple delays and some legal sparring over the trial's location, the proceedings commenced on August 1st in the Mill Creek Courthouse. On the day that Fred and Harley were scheduled to testify, Harley picked up Fred at the auto repair shop and Harley drove the 16 miles to Mill Creek. Fred proudly rode 'shotgun' and even had a pleasant conversation with Harley on the way to testify. After their mutual experience during the robbery attempt, Fred and Harley were now buddies and mostly enjoyed each other's company. After arriving at the courthouse, Fred noticed that most of the attendees were locals who were curious about the case, but one attendee bothered Fred. He was a big hairy man with multiple tattoos, two ear rings and a buzz cut. Fred estimated he was as tall as Charley and Harley and a hundred pounds heavier. He was wearing a white muscle t-shirt with a MS-13 tattoo on his right shoulder. As Harley was being cross-examined by the defense attorney, Harley became visibly annoyed by the line of questioning. The inexperienced attorney was trying to get Harley to admit to using unnecessary force to subdue the suspect.

"When you assaulted him, he was on the floor, defenseless; right?
"He hadda gun", replied Harley.

All of a sudden shots were fired in the direction of Harley and the judge. Fred turned to see the burly tattooed gunman firing in the direction of Harley. He was quickly subdued by two deputies and handcuffed. As he was escorted out of the courthouse, he was screaming and cursing about how he was going to kill Harley. No one was injured in the shooting, but the judge was visibly shaken and adjourned the trial until the next day.

On the ride home, Harley seemed to take the incident in stride; remarking that gunman was a bad shot.
"That dick couldn't shoot hisself."
Fred laughed in agreement.
Nothing much was said during the 16-mile drive back to the shop. Fred decided on his drive home that he would not mention the courthouse shooting, fearing it might upset his mother.

The next day Fred and Harley again made the trip to Mill Creek in hopes of finishing their part in the trial. Both Harley and Fred wrapped up their cross examinations and were excused by the judge. The next day, after the jury had rendered a unanimous guilty verdict on all counts, the judge sentenced the convicted murderer to life in prison without parole.

With all the positive publicity surrounding the trial and Fred's ability to organize the scheduling and record keeping, the brother's auto repair business was brisk. The brothers could no longer handle the increase in traffic, so they hired an additional full-time mechanic. Since Fred was to start school in two weeks, the brothers feared that without Fred, their business might deteriorate. The brothers knew they could never replace Fred, so they offered him a modest raise and a full-time position as shop manager, working weekends and after school. Fred knew he would need money to buy gas and maintain his truck in good working condition. Since Fred calculated he would need $40 per week for gas travelling back and forth to school, he was pleased to have a steady income during the school year. However, Fred's mind was focused elsewhere. He was visualizing that first day of school when he could show off his new (at least for Fred) truck.

After his Sunday shift, Fred cautiously drove home and immediately washed his truck. Fred always kept his truck spotless inside and out, but Monday was going to be special. The truck's paint job was nearly perfect and after waxing displayed like a new truck. On Monday morning, Fred made the 18-mile trip to Mill Creek and Tygart Valley High/Middle School, where he would begin his ninth-grade year in a school of roughly 200 students. As Fred drove into the parking area, his friends plus several students gathered around his truck. Some were excited to see Fred and some were excited to see the truck. Fred was now a local celebrity and it seemed that everyone wanted to be his buddy. During the second week of school, Fred noticed an unfamiliar face looking at his truck.

She was a tall slim girl with long lush auburn hair. Her name was Alice and she was a new student, who had transferred from Huttonsville High. She was the prettiest girl that Fred had ever seen.

Chapter 4

*A*lice was an only child who grew up on a farm north of Valley Head. Her dad worked the coal mines near Mill Creek and her mother Sarah, worked part time at Point Mountain Union Mission Church. They were a close-knit religious family, who regularly attended Sunday church services and other church events. Alice's parents had always wanted a large family and things appeared moving in that direction when tragedy struck. Soon after Alice was born, Sarah became pregnant with twins. However, fate intervened when complications arose during childbirth and the twins were stillborn, leaving Sarah unable to have additional children.

Alice, too young to perceive her parents grief, developed into a girly girl, who was conservative in her tastes and outlook. Adventurous she was not. Fishing, hunting and rafting were not in her playbook. With no siblings to play with, Alice spent the majority of her time playing with her favorite dolls, her dollhouse and her beloved dog Ralphie.

Ralphie was a rescue pup and a mix between a Pug and a Beagle (Puggle). He was brought into the family as a six-month-old puppy; a birthday present for a one-year-old Alice. Ralphie was an indoor dog with big dark eyes, a tan coat and a white cross on his chest. They bonded immediately, and as they both developed mentally and emotionally, their bond continued to strengthen. Ralphie matured into a small highly-intelligent dog that was a constant companion for Alice. They slept together, napped together and Ralphie was a comfort to Alice when she was sick or sad. In preschool, he was her best and only friend.

Alice attended Huttonsville Grade School and was well-liked by her classmates. Alice developed physically sooner than most girls and by the time she was 12 years old, she was being noticed by older boys. Alice was a tall slim curvy young woman who drew admiring glances from men of all ages. Even though she was a conservative dresser, her physical attributes were evident for all to see. As Alice entered sixth grade, jealousy raised its ugly head among some of her best girlfriends. The bullying started soon after and the unassuming Alice went from an outstanding student to one that barely tried. She started to hate school. After she was attacked, beaten and kicked in the hallway by three girls who had formerly been her friends, Alice's parents made the decision to transfer Alice to Mill Creek High/Middle School for her freshman year. More misery soon followed when her precious Ralphie became sick and died during the summer before school started. Alice was inconsolable and wept for days. Ralphie had been her constant companion for 14 years and their love for each other had never wavered. A few weeks later, a down-trodden Alice reluctantly began classes at her new school in Mill Creek. Initially, the girls in her classes were skeptical of this sad transfer student and largely avoided Alice. Many of the boys however, were eager to make her acquaintance, and most had one thing on their mind. The curvaceous teen was the talk of the boy's locker room and the subject of many crude jokes that circulated among teen-age boys. Alice's parents had not allowed her to date and she never had a boyfriend. Alice had always been an excellent student, but at her new school, her grades continued to suffer. One concerned English teacher offered to tutor her after school on Thursdays and Alice accepted. One Thursday, and after her tutoring session had ended early, Alice walked down the hall to use the ladies restroom. Her parents would be picking her up in 15 minutes, so Alice knew she would have plenty of time to freshen up. At this time of day, the school was mostly empty of students and teachers.

Fred was busy taking an unmonitored makeup test in a classroom across from the women's restroom. Fred's teachers trusted his honesty and often allowed him to take unmonitored exams. Suddenly Fred thought he heard muffled screams outside. When he heard them a second time, he decided to investigate. Once he was in the hallway, the bloodcurdling screams seemed to come from the nearby bathroom. Fred rushed inside to find Alice fighting for her life. The assailant had managed to rip off her skirt and remove her bra, exposing her ample bosom. She was being assaulted by the janitor. Fred jumped into action and grabbed the assailant by the neck and proceeded to pummel him with fists and elbows. Fred was short, but was a strong stocky teen who was used to schoolyard scraps and he had little trouble subduing the older janitor. Soon the assailant was bloodied and unconscious on the bathroom floor. Fortunately, Alice was not seriously hurt, but her clothes were torn and she was visibly shaken. She was also embarrassed that Fred had seen her partially naked. The commotion had drawn a small group of teachers, who were quick to call 911.
The assailant turned out to be a recently-hired 55-year-old, who was a registered pedophile with a long arrest record. While waiting for the authorities and Alice's parents, Fred put

his arm around Alice and tried to comfort her the best he could. However, it was Alice that noticed that Fred was the one that was hurt. Alice had always been terrified at the sight of blood.

"Oh my god, you're hurt," Alice screamed.
"I'm okay", assured Fred.
"But you're BLEEDING," cried Alice hysterically.

During his struggle to subdue the attacker, the janitor had pulled a knife and had plunged his blade deep into Fred's side. Fred had also been slashed across his upper arm. Blood was everywhere, but Fred barely noticed. He was too busy trying to comfort a sobbing Alice. When the sheriff and ambulance arrived, Fred and Alice were taken to The Davis Medical Center in Elkins and the janitor was arrested and taken to jail. Fred received a total of 30 stitches and was kept overnight as a precaution. Alice was released to her parents and even though Alice wanted to stay with Fred, her parents convinced her it was best to rest at home. It was the first time that Alice had noticed Fred at her new school in Mill Creek and marked the beginning of a remarkable relationship.

In a plea deal with the prosecuting attorney, the janitor eventually pleaded guilty to a sexual assault charge. The attempted murder charge was dropped and the janitor was sentenced to 15 years in prison. A fragile Alice was relieved that she wouldn't have to testify.

Chapter 5

*R*eturning to school after a brief recuperation period, Fred found himself to be not only a school celebrity but Alice's hero. He and Alice soon began spending their lunch breaks together and rapidly became best of friends. Fred was the companion that Alice needed in this vulnerable time in her life. Alice felt comfortable talking to Fred and he responded by being a great listener. Alice needed that special someone who would listen and sympathize with her suppressed fears and feelings. They were two 15-year-olds that truly enjoyed each other's company.

Since Alice's parents would not allow Alice to date until she was 16, Fred patiently resigned himself to being her confidant while counting the days until her next birthday. From that very first day that Fred saw Alice, he knew that she was the girl for him, and he wanted more than just being friends. Because Alice was not physically attracted to the shorter Fred, she desired only friendship. Her vision of the perfect boyfriend was the tall dark handsome type, and there were several eager older boys that fit that description. Fred knew that he needed a plan to secure the first date with Alice once she turned 16. He didn't intend to stand aside and let some older boy be the first one to date Alice. But first, he needed to gain her trust. In the weeks that followed, Alice began to reveal her innermost feelings to Fred.

During an early lunch break, Fred and Alice were able to secure a table for two in the school cafeteria. Alice was still reeling from the events of the previous months and she was feeling sad and lonely.

"I feel so alone," mumbled Alice as she looked down to avoid looking directly at Fred.
"No one understands me; not my parents; not my teachers; not my classmates."
She then gradually raised her head, and her bright, sparkling blue eyes stared intently at Fred.
"You are the only one who understands me."
Fred was startled upon hearing those words, but managed to reply, "Yes of course I understand you."
"After my Ralphie died, my heart ached and I felt so empty inside." As she spoke, her lower lip quivered as tears formed in her baby-blue eyes.
Fred became emotional, but was able to reassure her. "You're not alone, I'm right here with you."
At this time in her life, Alice badly needed a shoulder to lean on and Fred happened to be the right one in the right place at the right time.

Fred and Alice spent almost every lunch break together during their freshman year and Alice would continue to pour her heart out to Fred. As Fred began his sophomore year, school studies and his full-time job at the repair shop kept him busy, but never too busy to be with Alice when she needed him.

Fred was also busy devising a plan to celebrate their 16th birthdays by having a nice dinner at a newly-opened restaurant at the Snowshoe Resort. Fred hoped to be Alice's first date after she turned 16. He knew that plenty of older boys were salivating over the prospect of dating the slim, curvaceous Alice and Fred wanted to be first in line.

Their birthdays were one week apart and because Alice has made clear to Fred that she wants their relationship to be strictly platonic, Fred plans to make this dinner a celebration. He lays the groundwork by first gaining approval from Alice's parents. Fred plans to take Alice to the Appalachia Kitchen Restaurant in Snowshoe to celebrate their birthdays. Alice's parents obviously know of Fred and trust him to take good care of their daughter. After getting their consent, Fred must now convince Alice. A birthday celebration, not a date, assures Alice that this would be fun and she agrees. The Snowshoe Resort is 17 miles (28 minute drive) from Valley Head and Fred promises to have Alice home by 11 p.m.

The big night finally arrives and Fred appears at Alice's doorstep promptly at 6:30 p.m. His truck is spotless and he's wearing his Sunday best. During their drive to Snowshoe, Alice is upbeat, talkative and anxious to see the resort. Since she was not a skier, this visit to Snowshoe would be her first.

During dinner, Alice and Fred were both animated as they talked, laughed and thoroughly enjoyed each other's company. After they had finished their venison dinner, Fred's planned surprise was set in motion. Suddenly, several servers rushed in singing happy birthday while carrying a white round cake with 16 candles. The cake was inscribed with the words, *To Alice, Happy Birthday to my dream girl.* Her blue eyes glistened and Alice was overcome with emotion. After dinner and on the ride home, Alice was strangely quiet and thoughtful. Fred was concerned that maybe he had done something wrong, but hadn't a clue what it might be. Fred had Alice home a little before 11 p.m. Facing Alice and gazing into her clear blue eyes, Fred sought clues as to what to do next. He was standing on the first step while Alice stood on the ground. This made Fred feel slightly taller than Alice and made him feel comfortable in case a good night kiss was forthcoming. Fred didn't have to wait long as Alice took the initiative and kissed Fred squarely on the lips. It was a closed-mouth quick kiss, but was something that Fred had hoped for.

"Would you like to go out next Friday?" Fred asked.
"I'm sorry; I already have a date,"
Fred knew that Alice was only allowed to date on Friday nights, since Sunday morning church services were early and school nights were off limits.
"What about the next week?" Fred asked hopefully.
"Okay," said Alice and into her house she went.

The next two weeks passed slowly for Fred as he counted the days until his date with Alice. He planned to take her to a movie in Valley Head followed by treats at the local Dairy Queen. On the short ride to the theater in Valley Head, Alice seemed dejected and worried about something. They arrived several minutes early and it gave Fred a chance to find out what was troubling Alice.

"Are you okay?" inquired Fred.
After a long pause, Alice replied, "no, not really."
"What's wrong?"
"My date last weekend was a total nightmare. After a nice evening of bowling, my date expected me to have sex with him and he wouldn't take no for an answer."
"What did you do?"
"I got out of his car, ran to a nearby gas station and called my parents. My date drove off and I haven't seen him since. My parents were upset; I was upset: Fred, what's wrong with me?"

29

Fred assured her that she had done nothing wrong.
"You just had a bad date with a real jerk."
"Am I a bad judge of character?"
"You couldn't be, you're out with me. Aren't you?"
They both shared a good laugh and proceeded into the theater. The night ended again on Alice's doorstep. Fred took his position on the first step and this time Fred seized the opportunity to hold Alice close to him while giving her a long wet kiss. Alice seemed to participate willingly and afterwards Fred was so excited that he forgot to ask her for another date.

By Monday, Alice already had a date with a senior boy who happened to be captain of the football team and the most popular boy at school. Obviously Fred was disappointed, but managed to secure a date for the following Friday.

The following Friday, Fred was 10 minutes late due to a traffic accident on US Highway 19 and hurried to Alice's front door. As they walked back to Fred's truck, Fred could see that Alice was not her cheery self. Fred had planned a round of miniature golf and then hoped for some alone time with Alice. He was also keenly interested in knowing if Alice enjoyed her date with the football hero.

"Is there anything wrong?"
"Not really," replied Alice.
"How was your date with the football star?"
"I'd rather not talk about it."
"Okay, but you know you can always tell me anything."
Her bottom lip quivered as she looked squarely at Fred and quietly revealed; "I'm a virgin Fred, and I want to stay that way until I'm married. Saving myself for my husband is important to me and the boys I've been attracted to lately seem to want something different."
"I respect that," answered Fred.

"Are all boys that way?"

"I don't know about all boys, but this boy knows that you are my dream girl, and I would never do anything to hurt you or disrespect you."

"Thank you Fred."

Fred was also a virgin, but felt this was not the right time to tell Alice.

After a round of miniature golf, Alice continued to pour out her feelings to Fred. Her dream date with the football star had turned out badly before it even began. He had come to pick her up in his van, pointed out the bed in the back and let her know from the outset that he was only interested in one thing. Alice stormed out of the van and returned to her house confused and upset. However, Fred was relieved that the date went badly.

"What a jerk."

"Why are these guys so crude and disrespectful? Why can't they be more like you?"

"I don't know Alice, but let's talk about something else."

As Fred walked Alice hand in hand to her front door, he felt certain that he was the luckiest guy around.

As Fred faced Alice on the first step, he could feel his pulse quicken. He boldly pulled Alice close to him and as he kissed her, pulled her even closer with both hands squarely on her firm backside. His throbbing member pressed firmly against Alice as his tongue found hers and on that night their attraction became magical. This time Fred remembered to ask for another date. "Alice, will you go out with me next Friday?"

"I would love to," replied Alice. And so began a two-year courtship replete with an intensity that can only be enjoyed in the spring of life. Fred knew he had feelings for Alice, but still was unsure if she felt the same.

Chapter 6

Alice did eventually fall in love with Fred, in a way one falls asleep; slowly and then completely. As they headed toward their favorite parking spot on top of Pt. Mountain, Alice was looking forward to her weekly make out session with Fred. But for some unknown reason, she was uneasy of what lay ahead. The night was ominous with only a hint of moonlight shining through the cloud cover. They had been parked for about 15 minutes, but long enough to steam up the windows, when a knock on the driver side window interrupted the stillness of the night.

The last thing they expected on this cold dark night was a knock on the window. After a brief period to put their clothing in order, Fred slowly rolled down the window about two inches.

"Police, open up!" said a deep voice.

Before Fred could react, the window was shattered and two strong hands grabbed Fred by his shirt and pulled him out of the truck. The intruder then bashed Fred in the head with a crowbar knocking him unconscious. Before he could strike Fred again, Alice leaped into action and grabbed the intruder from behind and prevented what could have been a deadly second strike on the unconscious Fred. The intruder quickly subdued Alice and turned his attention to the truck. Fred had left the keys in the ignition and the assailant was off into the night.

As the truck sped off into the darkness, Alice tried to locate Fred. It was freezing on the mountain and was now pitch black. On her hands and knees, she moved toward the sound of Fred's labored breathing.
"Fred; Fred," she screamed.

The ground was cold and damp and Alice had only a sweater. Fred had left his jacket in the truck which was now rolling down the mountain. Alice knelt down beside Fred and tearfully prayed. After what seemed like an eternity, Fred regained consciousness.

"Oh my God, Fred, you're alive," sobbed a terrified Alice.

As Fred mumbled incoherently, Alice threw her body over him and made the wise decision to stay put until daylight. The two-mile trek down the mountain would have to wait.

Meanwhile, the parents had called 911 and reported Alice and Fred missing. The police were already looking for a convicted felon, who had escaped from the state pen in Huttonsville; they added Alice and Fred to their search. When Fred failed to show for work, Harley knew something was wrong; Fred never missed work and he was an hour late. Looking out the window, Harley saw Fred's red truck, but a stranger outside was filling the gas tank. Harley warily approached the stranger and bellowed.

"Whassup?"

"Where's Fred," Harley yelled.

Harley abruptly recognized the stranger. It was the same guy that had tried to kill Harley not once, but twice. The same guy who had been sentenced to life in prison three years earlier for murder and robbery.

What happened next was a fight scene rarely seen in the hills of West Virginia. Both men were roughly the same height, but this 'stranger' was 100 pounds heavier than Harley. With no weapons in sight, Harley approached the man with fists flying in every direction. What followed was a titanic struggle between two big men intent on total destruction. Witnessed by a handful of startled spectators, this fight had no rules. Biting, groin kicking and eye gouging were standard strategies used by both men in trying to subdue the other. The grunts and groans seemed to echo throughout the valley as the two giants struggled for dominance. Finally, Harley delivered a head butt that shattered the felon's nose; he followed that with an uppercut that staggered the man backwards. One more kick in the groin flattened his adversary and the fight seemed to be over, but not for Harley. The rage that had been inside Harley for years, poured out of him as he jumped on his helpless opponent, continuing to pummel him with elbows and fists. A couple of spectators finally pulled Harley off the man and the spectacle was over. The police were called and an ambulance carted off the big man who was barely alive. Harley was hurt, but refused aid, and called Charley instead. After convincing his brother to relieve him at the shop, Harley took the day off.

Meanwhile, Fred and Alice were struggling to descend the mountain. What would have normally taken an hour, took them three. Both were suffering from hypothermia and Fred was still dazed when they reached the paved road. After flagging down an 18-wheeler, Fred and Alice eventually made it to the hospital. Fred was treated for a concussion and given 25 stitches to his head. Alice suffered a fractured arm and both were treated for hypothermia. After several days of observation, both were discharged and allowed to go home. Fred returned to work the next day and was astonished to see his truck in front of the auto shop. Charley and Harley were both there to greet him. Harley excitedly explained to Fred in detail how his truck was recovered and gave Fred a 'blow by blow' description. They all shared a rare group hug and celebrated Fred's return over a cup of coffee.

The escaped felon recovered a few weeks later and was returned to prison. Ironically Fred, Alice and the felon were all treated in the same hospital.

Fred now had other things on his mind. Fred and Alice would graduate from high school in the spring and Fred was wanting to get married. Alice's parents were determined that Alice first earn a college degree and had secured enough money for her to attend WVU in Morgantown. After Alice promised to obtain her degree at a later date and after a very convincing Fred had asked for her hand in marriage, her parents reluctantly acquiesced. Alice's parents knew that Fred was smart, a hard worker, a devout Christian and would take good care of Alice. Fred made plans for a June wedding in the Pt. Mountain Union Mission Church followed by a honeymoon in Niagara Falls. Fred had saved enough money to pay for their airfare and a honeymoon suite. Exactly one week after their high school graduation, Fred and Alice were married. That afternoon they were flying to Niagara Falls. The happy couple had never been on a plane before and the ever cautious Alice was anxious. Fred held her hand for most of the flight.

They finally arrived in Niagara Falls and settled into their honeymoon suite soon after midnight. Neither was tired, but Fred was extremely excited. Gazing at Alice in her flimsy nightgown, he was able to see the voluptuous body of a fully developed beautiful young woman. Saving herself for marriage was important to Alice, but being a virgin was not exactly Fred's first choice, but she was his everything and in this moment Fred's desire was so strong he felt he might explode. And explode he did immediately upon entering Alice's silky smooth love box. She was worth the wait and on that night he would have to wait no longer, as he experienced this eruption time and time again. As you might expect, Fred's first attempt at lovemaking, even though short lived, was uncomfortable for Alice. With a little lubricant and an understanding Fred, Alice soon became a willing participant. The early morning hour found Alice on top of Fred with his member deep inside her. She slowly and deliberately moved up and down the length of his rock-hard manhood. She was becoming an enthusiastic participant moaning with each thrust. Her moans became louder as her stroking of Fred's member quickened. After a few minutes, Fred rolled over on top of Alice and began his powerful thrusts into her hidden treasure. Suddenly Alice responded with an increased intensity as Fred's large member probed the depths of her love tunnel. Her luscious lips, breasts and buttocks had previously been the subject of Fred's attention but now he was focused on thrusting his rock-hard organ into Alice with increased urgency. Fred was still plunging inside of her when she suddenly screamed.

"Oh my God Fred, Oh my God," she cried.

Alice was not in the throes of an orgasm, but instinctively was trying to help Fred climax and climax he did. Fred's sperm exploded deep inside her as his entire body tensed and then gradually relaxed in a pool of pleasure.

A square-jawed muscular young man with a fearless nature, Fred was shorter than his tall curvaceous wife, but during their magical honeymoon he felt 10 feet tall. Because their mutual affection was unrestricted, their initial experience at lovemaking contained all the elements of intimacy, passion and commitment. Over the next four days, Alice and Fred would have the time of their young sexual lives and this time together would bring them even closer as their love for each other deepened. Their time in Niagara Falls passed too quickly and they were soon on a plane back to West Virginia. It was the first time that either had been outside of WV and Fred sensed that Alice was more at ease with herself and her surroundings.

Fred's parents had arranged for the couple to stay rent-free in a newly-built cabin on their property west of the main house. The cabin had originally been built for members of their extended family to stay while visiting. The happy couple returned from their honeymoon late at night and proceeded down the ½ mile dirt road leading to the cabin. Alice barely noticed the bumpy road as she drove her new Honda Civic toward the dark cabin. She was having flashbacks of her ride up Pt. Mountain two years earlier, only this time there was no unwanted stranger. The Honda was a graduation present from Alice's parents and it made Fred and Alice a two-car family.

The well-built one-bedroom cabin had electricity, indoor plumbing and a nice stone fireplace, but no central heat and air. Once the couple got settled, the silent environment of the mountain worked its magic and they fell fast asleep.

Chapter 7

The 1990's ushered in a decade of peace and prosperity. The internet changed the way people work and play. And the cell phone changed the way people communicate. The lives of Alice and Fred were far removed from the Oklahoma City bombings, the Rodney King beating and the LA riots. They were able to enjoy the expanded use of the internet and the widespread utilization of cell phones.

The young couple settled into married life and totally enjoyed their time in the small cabin, but were soon eager to have their own home and start a family. They were a two-income family and were soon able to save enough money to build their dream home. Alice was working full-time at the Pt. Mountain Baptist Church and Fred's duties and income continued to increase as the Auto Repair Shop underwent a remarkable expansion. They decided to build a house just north of where Fred's parents lived and after two years of planning and construction, their house was finally completed and move-in ready. The newly-weds spared no expense in furnishing their new home with the latest appliances and decor. Once Fred and Alice were settled in their modern three-bedroom house, the twenty year-olds made plans to expand their family. But first, Fred surprised Alice and brought home another Puggle rescue puppy. Fred knew he would never be able to replace Ralphie, but hoped that Alice would find comfort with her new companion. Alice was not only pleased, but was overwhelmed with emotion.

"She is beautiful", Alice sobbed through tears of joy. "The best surprise ever."
"I will name her Daisy, because she is beautiful and delicate; just like a flower in spring."

Fred then embraced Alice and gave her a long affectionate hug.

"I love you Alice. You will always be my dream girl."

The next three years contained intermittent periods of celebration and heartache. Alice suffered through two miscarriages and in her third pregnancy developed a condition called preeclampsia (a condition marked by high blood pressure and possible kidney damage), which typically puts both the baby and mother at high risk. Both Alice and Fred wanted a large family and Alice especially wanted a baby girl. But despite prayer and guidance from the area's best doctors, their prayers were not answered. Because of Alice's bout with preeclampsia, her baby was delivered stillborn and Alice spent two weeks in ICU and another two months recovering physically. Doctors had to tell Fred the bad news that Alice would be unable to bear children in the future and was extremely lucky to be alive.

Despite losing their dream of a large family, their love for each other remained unshakable. As their dream of having their own children faded, they became increasingly involved in the activities of the church and eventually explored the difficult process of adoption. Endless paperwork and regulatory procedures followed with no end in sight. Countless disappointments were followed by false hope and Fred and Alice were gradually losing the expectation that a successful adoption was in their future.

And then a miraculous opportunity developed in their Pt. Mountain Church community. An unmarried 16 year-old church member, with an unwanted pregnancy, desired that a church member adopt her unborn child. The girl had been brutally raped by a college basketball player while on spring break. The girl's father was an elderly single parent who had neither the resources nor the desire to take care of his grandchild. The girl had no other family members. Since the rapist was convicted and serving time in prison, his parental rights had been terminated. The girl knew that Fred and Alice were trying to adopt and could and would provide an excellent home for her child. Even so, overcoming the legal hurdles that would surely lie ahead appeared to be challenging. But after several agonizing months, their prayers were answered when the church attorney intervened. He happened to be an expert in adoption procedures involving infants born to under-age victims of rape or incest, and volunteered his services. With the help of this shrewd attorney, Fred and Alice were able to legally adopt a healthy infant within days of her birth. Needless to say, Alice and Fred were thrilled to welcome this baby girl into their family.

They named her MacKenzie after Alice's Scottish grandmother.

Chapter 8

Alice and Fred had gone to great lengths to decorate and furnish an entirely pink bedroom just for Mackenzie. Alice and Fred were obviously excited to welcome their newborn into their home, but maybe not as excited as Daisy. With her tail wagging wildly, the young puppy was barely able to control herself as she sniffed and pranced while welcoming this tiny baby girl to her new home. The addition of another family member was a defining moment in the lives of Fred and Alice, but little did they know of the joy and life-changing heartbreak their new addition would bring.

At bedtime, MacKenzie, Fred and Alice would share their king-size bed while Daisy slept on the floor in her own puppy bed. As the days grew into weeks and then months, Fred and Alice began to realize that their baby was special. She had always been an alert and curious baby, but Mac began walking at seven months and soon thereafter was talking in full sentences. By the time she was two, Mac had an extensive vocabulary that was bolstered by watching television, particularly the news. Her recall was extraordinary and Alice suspected she had a photographic memory. At two years of age Mac and Daisy moved into their own pink bedroom. At age three, Mac was reading books of all types, but her favorites were historical nonfiction and biographies. She especially enjoyed her weekly trips to the local library and would spend hours there if her mother would let her.

But there was something else, Mac was also very strong and coordinated for her age. After a regular yearly visit with the pediatrician, Alice and the doctor had a hushed conversation about Mac. Alice feared the worst and nervously listened to the deliberate words of the pediatrician.

"I have never encountered a 4-year-old with the physical and mental acuity of your daughter. Not only does she measure off the charts intellectually, but her strength and coordination are astonishing."

A relieved Alice responded, "You mean that there is nothing wrong with her and she is a normal baby."

"No, that is not what I'm saying. What I'm saying is that she is exceptional. She is extraordinarily gifted. Her IQ is so high, it cannot be measured; her athletic gifts are incredible. She also is very alert, curious and I suspect has a photographic memory."

Alice was both stunned and relieved. She had worried that her displays of intellect might signal something amiss with her development. When Mac returned from the examination room, Alice could not hold back her tears.

"What's wrong, Mama´?"
"Nothing's wrong; I'm just happy and I love you so much."

"I love you too, Mama."

The bond between Alice and Mac was also exceptional. Mac seldom needed correcting, but when she did, it was always, yes mama, and she seldom needed to be told a second time. Their love was mutual and Mac always wanted to please her mama. However, Fred was Mac's regular playmate. Ball throwing, ball kicking, checkers, board games and cards were games that Fred and Mac both enjoyed. Of course Mac loved Fred, but not the same as her mama. She was definitely a mama's girl. And then there was Daisy. Daisy and Mac were constant companions. Mac walked Daisy, fed Daisy and cuddled regularly with her furry companion. Mac was a happy child who relished her pre-school childhood.

"Mama, can Daisy go to church with us?"
"No, dear. Dogs are not allowed in church."
"Why Mama? Daisy will be quiet and won't cause trouble."
"That may be true but not all dogs are like Daisy, and if the church allows just one dog, they will have to allow others."
"Ok Mama, I know she will be lonely, but I will make sure to play extra with Daisy when we get home."

Church-going at Pt. Mountain Baptist Church was a regular Sunday activity and even though she missed Daisy, she cherished the singing, seeing all the people, and sometimes even the sermon.

Mac was an active child and was constantly wanting to play outside. In Alice's view, playing outside was a dangerous activity for a preschooler and would only allow it if Alice was part of the outdoor session. When Mac was five, she looked forward to her daily outdoor activities. She liked throwing rocks in the Tygart River and picking elderberries on her uncle's farm.

One day Mac was watching her favorite history channel and during a commercial break, she happened onto a sports channel that was showing the 1999 Women's U. S. Open Tennis Final. Mac was fascinated by the play of 18-year-old Serena Williams, who went on to win her first U. S. Open Crown. The athleticism, power and shot-making ability of Williams, plus the enthusiasm of the pro-Williams crowd, ignited an excitement in Mac that inspired this reaction.

"Mama, I want to play tennis."
"Ok, we'll see."
"But mama, I really want to play. When can I start?"
"Let me talk to you father and see what he thinks. Ok?"

But Mac couldn't wait, she immediately ran out on the porch where Fred was quietly eating a fresh peach.

Mac shouted, "Dad, can I play tennis?"
Even though Fred didn't know anything about tennis, he responded, "Let me talk to your uncle Henry; I believe he knows how to play."
"Ok daddy, I can hardly wait to try it."

Fred loved his peaches and could be frequently found on summer afternoons, carving slices of a ripe peach with his pocket knife. Fred paid no attention to the occasional yellow jacket landing on a freshly-cut peach slice. He would just calmly bring the slice to his mouth and the bee would fly harmlessly away. As far as Mac knew, her father had never been stung, but Mac was fearful of yellow jackets because her mother had warned her that they could easily sting if disturbed.

Two weeks later, Mac heard a knock on the front door. It was Uncle Henry with a large wrapped package.
"Mac, I have a present for you."
"You have? What is it? Can I open it now?"
"Sure can."

Mac excitedly began unwrapping her present. By the time Mac opened the box, she was joined by Fred, Alice and Daisy.

"Wow, is this for me?"

Inside was an adult-sized, brand-new tennis racquet with three new Wilson tennis balls. Even though, the racquet was too big and the handle too large, that mattered little to Mac, as she was ready to try out her new racquet and balls in the house.

Alice quickly intervened. "No Mac. Not in the house."
"Then where can I play?" Mac replied in a concerned voice.
"Outside."
"OK, Mama."

Mac and Daisy were quickly out the door, followed by Alice, Fred and Henry. From the porch, Mac was occasionally able to hit the ball into the yard. When she connected, Daisy was right there to retrieve the ball and bring it back to the porch.

After a few minutes, Henry joined in and said.

"There's a nice spot over yonder by our barn. Tomorrow she can hit on the barn door."

The next morning Mac was ready to play tennis. She carried one ball, her racquet and was followed by Daisy and Alice. Even though the 100-yard dirt path walk was familiar to Mac, Alice insisted on going with them; at least for the first time.

Henry had painted a white line 3 feet from the ground on the barn door and a bulls-eye 3 feet above the line. Mac's first attempts to hit the ball toward the barn door were frustrating, but she did improve. Daisy turned out to be a reliable helper by retrieving every errant ball and returning it to Mac.

After an hour, Alice was ready to go home, but Mac wanted more time to practice. "Can I play just five more minutes?"

"Ok, honey, but only five minutes."

On the way home, Mac was animated. "That was fun. I don't think I was very good in the beginning, but I did get better. I can't wait to try again tomorrow."

And so began a summer of playing tennis against Henry's barn door, throwing rocks in the Tygart River, picking wild elderberries and playing catch with Daisy. Mac loved her mother's elderberry pies and her favorite sandwich was peanut butter and elderberry jelly. Of course Mac still found time to read her favorite books and attend church on Sundays.

Chapter 9

*A*s Mac's summer came to an end, she prepared for a brand new challenge; her first day of school at Mill Creek Elementary. Since her IQ scores were so high, it was recommended to Alice and Fred that Mac skip kindergarten and start school in the first grade.

"Mama, will there be a lot of people there? And will my teachers be nice?" Alice reassuringly answered. "Honey, you will enjoy school, you will learn new things and make some wonderful friends."

Despite her mother's comforting words, Mac was strangely nervous. She was tightly holding her mother's hand as she approached the school's front door. There they were met by the school Principal, Mr. Hansen, who had a friendly smile and offered to take Alice and Mac to her classroom and meet her teacher. It seemed that her classmates were already seated when Mac, Alice and Mr. Hansen entered the classroom. There was one vacant seat in the front of the class and even though there were only 12 students, Mac figured there were twice that number. After shaking hands with Mrs. Harper and taking the front-row seat, Mac took time to study her first-grade teacher. She was a portly middle-aged woman, who was all smiles and on the surface seemed very nice. Her stylish rimless glasses covered bright hazel eyes and her perfectly-groomed short gray hair completed the picture of a first-rate teacher. Mac listened to every word that her teacher uttered and was impressed with her command of English. Mac had never heard anyone who could express themselves so clearly. The first few days Mac was content to listen, but it wouldn't take long before Mac would begin raising her hand to ask questions.

"Mrs. Harper, your English is so good; where did you learn to speak so clearly?" The class let out a collective giggle, which embarrassed Mac, but Mrs. Harper promptly answered.

"I grew up in Columbus, Ohio and went to a strict Catholic school. The nuns insisted that I speak clearly and express myself in a way that could be easily understood. It is my hope that in this class, we can all do the same."

As the days turned into weeks, Mac could sense that Mrs. Harper's patience was wearing thin with the conduct of a portion of the class (mostly boys) who were misbehaving. On several occasions, a mean streak would surface that scared Mac. Mrs. Harper always held a ruler in her hand and would smack it against her palm when she was irritated. Mac imagined that 50 years earlier, nuns may have smacked the back of Mrs. Harper's hands when she was misbehaving.

After several weeks, Mac adjusted nicely to Mrs. Harper's rules and for the most part enjoyed class, particularly coloring. However, her favorite activities were lunch and recess. She loved playing outside with the other kids and made great use of all the playground equipment. She had no trouble using the parallel bars and with some effort could even do a pull-up. Each recess would end with a race around the playground and Mac was always the first to finish.

During cold weather, recess was held in the gym, where Mac was first introduced to basketball. After a couple of basketball sessions, Mac was able to dribble equally-well with her left and right hand. She was also able to regularly make baskets on the ten-foot hoop. Her teachers were so impressed with her basketball skills that they would sometimes let Mac play with the third and fourth graders.

During the summer months, Mac always found some time to practice tennis against her uncle's barn door. On this bright sunny spring morning, Mac was wearing her new tennis dress, white tennis shoes and had her silky auburn hair drawn in a neatly-combed pony tail. Alice had agreed to let Mac and Daisy make the 100 yard trek to her uncle's barn by themselves on the condition that Mac would be back in one hour. Alice had given Mac a Timex watch for just that purpose. It was 12 noon and the scent of wildflowers filled the air as Mac and Daisy began their short trek to Henry's barn. Having just completed first grade, the 6-year old was anxious to play some tennis. Playing tennis during the school year was difficult because it was generally dark by the time Mac returned home from school. On this morning, Alice decided to let Mac and Daisy make the 100-yard walk to their uncle's barn by themselves.

Suddenly, Mac heard something in the grass just behind her. Daisy had seen the snake first and in a valiant effort to protect Mac was bitten on the face by a 4-foot timber rattlesnake. Daisy's head swelled almost immediately to twice its size and Mac instinctively rushed into action. She scooped up Daisy and began running back to the house, yelling, "Mama, Mama, Daisy is hurt." Upon hearing Mac screaming her name, Alice and Fred met them at the front door.

"What happened Mac?"
"I think Daisy was bitten by a snake."
Mac's baby-blue eyes were filled with tears as she anxiously asked, "Mama, will Daisy be okay?"
"I hope she will be. Let's get her in the car and we can take her to the vet."

Fred blurted out. "I'll go see if I can find the snake."

During the 15-minute drive to the vet, Mac did her best to comfort Daisy. Upon arrival at the veterinarian and after a brief examination of Daisy, the doctor asked Alice if she knew what kind of snake had bitten Daisy. Before Alice could answer, Fred rushed into the examination room with a dead snake.
"I think this is the one that bit Daisy."

Mac confirmed that it looked like the same snake. The doctor quickly identified the snake as a timber rattlesnake and fortunately had some anti-venom in the office. Thirty minutes after receiving the medication, Daisy seemed to perk up slightly. Her head was still swollen, but the doctor assured Mac that the swelling would subside in a couple of days.

During Daisy's recovery, Mac stayed by her side and tended to her every need. When Mac was in school, it became Alice's turn to watch over Daisy. The only time Daisy was left alone were the two hours the family attended Sunday church services. Once Daisy had fully recovered, Mac was ready to resume her regular tennis practices, but remained concerned about Daisy's safety on the short walk to her uncle's barn. The doctor had assured Mac and her parents that a future encounter with a venomous snake was highly unlikely. His words were fresh in Mac's mind.

"Stay on the dirt path and avoid rocks and logs where snakes might be hiding. Your dog has learned a hard lesson and will likely stay far away from snakes in the future."

After some serious discussions about safety, Alice finally agreed to allow Mac and Daisy to travel to her uncle's barn for some tennis practice, but only if Alice went along. Mac noticed that Daisy, who was 11 years old was starting to have trouble keeping up. Two weeks later she died a natural death. Mac was devastated and would take some time before resuming tennis practice on her uncle's barn door.

Chapter 10

$\mathcal{L}$oved by both her teachers and peers, Mac began second grade at Mill Creek Elementary looking forward to any challenges that might lie ahead. Even though she was both a kind and humble person, she was also endowed with a competitive streak that burned deep inside her. Mac always strived to be the best in everything.

Her talents as a basketball player did not take long to emerge. She could dribble with either hand and regularly make baskets inside of 15 feet. Occasionally her coaches would allow the 7-year-old to play with the fifth and sixth graders. During team games, she would usually be the high scorer and dominate play around the basket. As she grew older, she would always be the high scorer and her teammates grew irritated at her dominance. There was some bullying from the older girls and

Mac felt she was no longer liked by her basketball-playing teammates. In the fourth grade, she told her mother about her concerns.

"Mama, why do they hate me? We win almost every game."
"Maybe you should pass the ball to your teammates more."
"But they can't catch the ball and when they do they hardly ever make a basket."
"Honey, I think you should give it a try and maybe they will improve."
"Okay, Mama, I will pass a lot more."

So Mac surprised both her coaches and her teammates by making a concerted effort to distribute the basketball. At first, the players would be fooled by her passes and would seldom be ready to catch the ball; but as time went on, Mac's teammates improved and the bullying subsided. Meanwhile, Mac continued to excel in all subjects in the classroom. On standardized tests, she rarely missed, always scoring in the 99th percentile. Mac's highest scores were in reading comprehension, but math was a close second. School officials informed Fred and Alice that Mac had scored higher than anyone in Mill Creek Elementary history. During her fifth and sixth grade years, the Mill Creek girls' team never lost and the accolades for Mac increased with every win. High School coaches drooled over the prospect of having Mac enter the seventh grade and joining the High School team.

But Mac still dreamed of Wimbledon glory and continued to practice on her uncle's barn door. One day Mac saw an article in the Charleston Gazette about a 12-and-under girl's tennis tournament to be held at the Charleston Tennis Club. The tournament was scheduled for the July 4th weekend. Even though Mac had never played anyone in a match, much less a tournament, she knew the rules and longed to try her skills in a competitive environment.

"Mama, can I play in a tennis tournament in Charleston?"
"I don't think so honey, you've never played anyone before."
"But I know how to keep score and I don't miss very often when I practice."
"Let me discuss it with your dad first."
"Okay, but the entries close next week."
"I will talk to your dad tonight."

When Fred came home from work, Mac couldn't wait and rushed to her dad and blurted out.

"Dad, can I play in a tennis tournament in Charleston?"

Fred and Alice did have some shopping to do in Charleston and after some discussion, agreed to let Mac play in the tournament.

The big day finally arrived and Mac was super excited. Her first round match at the Charleston Tennis Club was scheduled at 9 a.m., which meant leaving Valley Head at 6. Mac was up and awake at 4:30. She combed her silky auburn hair in a fancy ponytail, dressed in her only tennis outfit and was ready to leave at 5:30. She was too keyed up to eat breakfast, but Alice insisted she eat something, so Mac reluctantly had a scrambled egg, toast and orange juice. On the 3-hour ride to Charleston, Mac was talkative, and couldn't wait to get there.

"Dad, how much longer?" To Mac, the drive seemed to take forever, but they managed to arrive a half-hour early.

To Mac's eyes, the Tennis Club was like Candy Land and Disneyland all wrapped in a single package. She carefully surveyed the manicured clay courts and the crowd of players, officials and spectators. She warily approached the tournament desk to check in and after showing her player's card, was given a can of new balls and assigned to court #9. Her first-round opponent was an 11-year old from Charleston and a novice player like Mac. After a shaky start, Mac won 7-5, 6-1. Her opponent was very nice and there were no controversies throughout the one-hour, player-umpired match. When the match was over, they hugged each other at the net and found ways to compliment each other's play.

Mac excitedly exclaimed to her mom after the match. "That was really fun. I think I got better the longer we played."

In Mac's second round match, she was paired with Emma Jones, the 12-and-under Ohio Valley champion from Dayton, Ohio. Emma was a mature, strong youngster, who was about the same height as Mac, but more developed physically.

Before the match, and unbeknownst to Mac, Emma had endured a tongue-lashing from her father, who was unhappy with her first round result. Even though Emma had won, her father was steamed and tore into Emma after the match.

"After everything your mom and I have sacrificed for you; the money we spent; lessons; academies; travel and you played like an idiot. In your next match, you had better be a lot better or there'll be hell to pay."
Emma and Mac were assigned the stadium court and the match began with Emma quickly winning the first set 6-0, but there was no quit in Mac. Mac was slowly learning to slide on

the green Har-Tru courts and was putting more and more balls in play. She hustled her way to 5-5 score in the second set and seemed ready to forge ahead 6-5 when an excellent forehand by Mac was called out. Because it was a second round match, there were still no umpires and players were calling their own lines. Mac, who was both a fiery competitor and very fair, expected the same from others. Emma had made several close out calls earlier in the match that appeared to be in, but Mac figured that they were just mistakes in judgment and did not question them. However this particular forehand was well inside the line and Mac felt strongly that she was being cheated. Mac approached the net and in a strong voice declared, "That ball was clearly in."

Even though it's against the rules of tennis to be on your opponent's side of the court, Emma quickly marched up to the net and proceeded to walk around the net post to confront Mac.
"Are you calling me a cheater?"

"I am," responded Mac. Her piercing blue eyes burned with an intensity that few have known or encountered, and she was not afraid of a confrontation and this is what her opponent was about to get.

Emma glared at Mac and uttered, "You're nothing but a country hick from West Virginia" Mac's eyes narrowed as she calmly declared, "What did you say?"

"You heard me. I said you were a country hick…"

Before she could finished, Mac unleased a straight right that would have made Mike Tyson proud. The punch knocked

Emma to the ground and bloodied her nose. The roughly dozen spectators let out a collective groan, "OOOh."

Alice, Fred and Emma's parents, who had been casually watching from the stands, were engaged in a friendly conversation when the blowup occurred. All four parents immediately rushed onto the court in an effort to comfort their daughters. Emma's dad, who was both a hothead and champion wrestler in high school, was particularly steamed and demanded that Fred do something to control and punish his daughter. Heated words were exchanged and soon fists were flying. The women were not to be left out and were soon involved in their own wrestling match, complete with hair-pulling, clawing and punching. Tournament officials eventually responded and order was somewhat restored.

Alice embraced a tearful Mac, who sobbed, "I'm sorry Mama, but she was trying to cheat me." That remark caused Emma's dad to blow his stack and he glared at Mac. "My daughter is not a cheat." He then demanded that tournament officials should never allow Mac to play junior tennis again, ever. Ultimately, the United States Tennis Association (USTA) did give Mac a six-month suspension for her part in the flare-up.

Meanwhile, an interested spectator, who had been observing this chaotic scene from afar, followed Mac and her parents to the parking lot where Fred's truck was parked. "Excuse me", he said. "My name is Scott Flannigan and I'm the Charleston Tennis Club's Director of Tennis. I observed your daughter's match with great interest and was impressed not only with her talent and athleticism, but with her focus and competitive spirit. If you are interested, I would be willing to help her achieve her potential as a tournament player and arrange to give her a weekly one hour lesson. I can also make arrangements for her to play here at the Club after her training session. The charge would be $60 for a one hour lesson with unlimited play on the day of her lesson."

Fred thanked him for the offer, but declined the invitation, saying that his daughter was through with tennis and would focus instead on her schoolwork and basketball.

On the long three-hour drive back to Valley Head, a still-distraught Mac was remorseful and continued to beg her mother to forgive her.

"I'm sorry Mama. I really am."

"It's okay, honey, I forgive you. You were put in a difficult situation and responded in a way you felt was justified. Your dad and I were no better in our actions. In fact, your dad and I are proud of you for standing up for yourself. It took courage to deal with what we all agree was an unpleasant situation." After a long pause, Alice said, "Why don't we stop and get some ice cream."

Fred who was nursing a bloody lip, chimed in, "That's the best idea I've heard today."

Chapter 11

Three weeks after the tournament's conclusion, Fred and Alice received a letter from the USTA informing them of their decision to suspend Mac from all sanctioned tournament play for six months. Hoping that Mac was no longer interested in playing tournaments, they said nothing to Mac about the letter. Mac, however, continued to hit daily on her uncle's barn door. She began practicing drills she had seen on YouTube and in the process developed flat controlled ground strokes. Mac was not one to be discouraged from following her dreams and when she had a goal, she was relentless in pursuing it. Her dream was Wimbledon glory and quitting tennis never entered her mind.

In the fall, she started Middle School. High School coaches recruited Mac and several of her seventh grade classmates to join the Tygart Valley High School team. After a month of practice the seventh graders were beating the juniors and seniors regularly in practice and despite being double-teamed and triple-teamed, Mac dominated the stat sheet. She led all players in scoring, rebounding and assists. When the season began, the starting five included three seventh graders, one senior and Mac.

Their first game was against Class AA powerhouse Elkins High School. Elkins was only a 25 minute drive from Mill Creek and since there were few Class A schools within 2 hours of Mill Creek, Tygart Valley was forced to schedule some class AA schools. Elkins had 900 students in grades 9-12 and Tygarts Valley had just under 200 in grades 7-12. Even though they had never beaten a team from Elkins, Mac and the entire team were looking forward to playing an actual game, instead of practicing among themselves. When the team bus set out for Elkins, it was 4 p.m. and just below freezing in early December. The winding mountain roads were icy and treacherous, but the weather had no impact on the mood of the players, as they laughed and sang during most of the trip.

Upon arrival in Elkins, they were in awe of the school and its facilities. The gym was packed with boisterous fans which included Fred, Alice and most of the team's parents. The Tygart Valley team got off to a good start as Mac scored the first two points and the team temporarily held their only lead of the game. The final score, won by Elkins was 72-36. Mac dominated the game for Tygart Valley and recorded a triple double (22 points, 12 rebounds and 12 assists). After the game a downcast Mac was disappointed with the result. She had given her all, but it was not enough. Mac was not used to placing second and the loss bothered Mac more than her teammates. The mood of the Tygart Valley coaches was just the opposite. The year before the team had been beaten 86-10 and the coaches were jubilant over the one-year improvement. The Tygart Valley team split the remaining 22 games to finish with a won-loss record of 11-12. It was the best record in Tygart Valley basketball history. Mac led the team in all categories and remained popular with teammates and coaches.

After Mac's 7th grade school year had ended, Mac was anxious to start playing tennis again and pursue her goal of winning Wimbledon. Mac was smart enough to know she needed professional coaching to achieve that goal. But first, she would have to convince her mom and dad to make a call to the tennis pro at the Charleston Tennis Club and see if the opportunity to improve her tennis through instruction and play was still available.

"Mama, can you call the Charleston Tennis Club Pro and see if he will still give me lessons?"
"No honey, your dad and I agreed that there would be no more tennis."
"But Mama, I have learned my lesson, I promise to be on my best behavior with no more outbursts."
"I'm sorry, but you need to concentrate on basketball and your school work and forget tennis."
"Please Mama, will your talk to dad?"
"Okay, but you know your dad; once he's made up his mind, it can be difficult for him to change."

That evening after dinner, Mac overheard her mom and dad discussing a possible return to tennis. She could tell that her dad was firmly against the idea. He had witnessed Mac's first tournament and that was enough for him. Later that evening Mac tried to persuade her dad to give her another chance at tennis.

"Please dad, I have learned my lesson and there will no more problems with my behavior from now on."
"No Mac, you are done with tennis."
Her big blue eyes filled with tears as she pleaded for another chance. "Please dad, I can and will do much better; you will be proud of me."
Grudgingly, Fred murmured: "Well, I will call him tomorrow."
Mac was elated, she brushed back her tears, tightly hugged her dad and cried out. "I love you daddy and I won't disappoint you."

The next day Fred called the Charleston Tennis Club and asked to speak with Scott Flannigan. He was told that Scott would be giving lessons all afternoon, but would return the call the next day. Scott remembered Mac and the incident a year earlier and told Fred he would need to talk to the Tennis Committee to see if they would okay Mac's return to the Club. Three weeks later, Scott called back and informed Fred that the Committee decided by a 3-2 vote to allow Mac to take lessons and play at the Club one day a week. Mac would be on probation and any bad behavior would result in the negation of all privileges at the Club. Mac plus one adult would also be allowed to order lunch in the Club's restaurant. Scott also informed Fred that the two negative Committee votes came from nationally-ranked senior players, who strongly objected to allowing Mac's return.

After thanking Scott, Fred asked: "When can she start?"
"She can start next week; I have Thursday available at 9 a.m."

"We will be there."

Alice and Mac arrived promptly at 9 a.m. on Thursday and Mac was more than ready to start training.

During the first lesson, it was obvious to Scott that Mac was more than just a world-class athlete. She was a listener, with a great attitude and a willingness to learn. The first thing Scott noticed was that the racquet Mac was using was an inexpensive racquet strung with a cheap nylon string. He escorted Mac over to the Pro Shop and they both selected a top-of-the-line Wilson demo racquet strung with Luxilon polyester. He also instructed Mac on the benefit of regularly using sunscreen during the hot summer months. Once they were back on the court, Scott discovered that Mac was ambidextrous and could serve equally well right or left handed. During their first lesson, Scott showed Mac how to hit slice, topspin and flat on her serve. He also showed her the proper grip (continental) and the importance of pronation. He even showed her how to practice her serve on a wall (or in Mac's case; a barn door).

After Mac's hour lesson, Mac and Alice sat on a wooden bench beside court #1 and talked about her lesson and the learning opportunity that had been gifted to Mac. They discussed the demo racquet, string and the tennis dresses that had caught Mac's eye. Mac and Alice both examined the demo racquet that Scott had loaned her for the day. By mid-morning, a senior player asked Mac if she would like to hit some; of course Mac enthusiastically responded: "Yes, I would love to." The senior was a woman who Mac judged to be in her sixties and she was quite good. After some spirited hitting, they both were upbeat and made a date to play again the following week. Mac and Alice then enjoyed a nice Caesar salad lunch on the Club veranda. As Mac and Alice gazed over the beautifully-maintained Club facilities, they marveled at the view. The outdoor restaurant overlooked the Club complex, which featured 9 outdoor Har-Tru (clay) courts, 2 hard courts, 6 indoor courts, 6 outdoor pickleball courts, a swimming pool, snack bar, fitness center and hiking trail. The Club was truly a world-class facility and the top private tennis club in West Virginia. During an eighteen-year period from 1970 to 1988, the Club hosted the National Girl's Sweet 16 Championships and tennis stars Tracy Austin and Chris Evert were both tournament winners. Mac figured that if they played at the Charleston Tennis Club and won Grand Slam titles, she could do the same. Mac began lessons at the Club in 2006 and the 13-year-old was oblivious to the hurdles and heartbreak that would lie ahead; obstacles that would undermine her chances at Wimbledon glory.

After lunch Mac was asked by a senior male if she would like to play a match. Of course Mac accepted. During the match, he ran Mac all over the court with an assortment of slices, angles, lobs and drop shots. In addition he gave Mac several bad calls while winning 6-1, 6-2. Mac said nothing about the bad calls and was gracious after the match. She even asked if he would show her how to hit a drop shot. It wasn't until some weeks later that Mac discovered that he was one of the Nationally-ranked seniors who had voted against allowing her to play at the Club. She guessed that his line-calling was an attempt to get a negative reaction.

Before the day was over, Alice would purchase a new racquet and tennis dress for Mac's birthday. It was 9 pm before Alice and Mac returned to Valley Head and Mac was anxious to tell her dad all about her day in Charleston. Fred listened intently and then hustled Mac off to bed.

The next day Mac was off to her uncle's barn to practice what she had learned the day before. She meticulously marked off the 39 feet from the barn door to an imaginary baseline which she drew with a stick in the dirt. From behind the baseline, she practiced her serve; both right-handed and left-handed. She tried to practice all the spins that Scott had showed her and in the process wished that she still had Daisy to play with and to chase errand balls. The summer break from school allowed Mac to engage in a variety of outdoor activities other than tennis. Mac enjoyed running, throwing rocks in the Tygart River, climbing trees and running barefoot in grass covered with white clover. Even though she had suffered a bee sting on the bottom of her foot as an 8-year-old, that didn't stop one of her favorite pastimes. But she was constantly on the alert for snakes and bees, by virtue of Alice's frequent warnings.

Chapter 12

The start of 8th grade came much too early for Mac, but she embraced the new school year with the same zest for learning that had always been her trademark. She was also anxious to continue the basketball success that she and her classmates had enjoyed as 7th graders. One big change was the attention she was getting from older boys. Mac was a beautiful young woman and the 11th and 12th grade boys were rapidly noticing this curvy, tall teen. With big blue eyes and silky auburn hair, which was most always drawn to a tight pony tail. Mac possessed a star quality that was acknowledged by all that knew her. Mac was unaffected by the attention and maintained a humility and kindness that was the essence of her personality. She was a modest, outgoing young lady and would remain that way for the rest of her life. At this stage of her life, she had little interest in boys and was motivated by learning new things and improving all facets of her life. And that included perfecting her skills in basketball and tennis. During Mac's 8th grade year, the Tygart Valley girls' basketball team posted a won-lost record of 15-8; the best in school history against mainly Class AA and Class AAA schools. Mac made honorable mention on several WV Class A All-State teams and again averaged a triple double, despite being regularly double and triple-teamed. Her 8th grade teammates also showed big improvements as the team averaged 65 points per game. Mac was happy because her teammates, coaches and school administrators were happy.

In the spring, Mac restarted her weekly tennis lessons at the Charleston Tennis Club. Scott had saved her 9 a.m. Thursday lesson time and looked forward to working with Mac's unique talent. After a 9-month school term, Scott expected Mac to be rusty, but was amazed at how much she had improved. During her first session back, Mac, remembering how effective the drop shot was used against her by the nationally-ranked senior, asked Scott to show her the proper way to hit a drop shot. Mac almost immediately was able to duplicate the shot off both wings; right or left handed. After several sessions, Scott recommended to Alice that Mac should play some state and sectional level junior tournaments outside of WV in order to facilitate her development. With the exception of an occasional D-1 male player, Mac was easily beating all comers at the Club.

After some lengthy discussions, Alice and Fred aligned their schedules and agreed to take Mac to play in 4 sectional level tournaments. One in June, two in July and one in August. All tournaments were less than a day's drive from Valley Head and were located in VA and KY. Alice would accompany Mac on two and Fred the other two. Of course, Mac was ecstatic and counted the days until the first tournament in Lynchburg, VA.

After an early start and a 3-hour drive to Lynchburg, Mac and Alice finally arrived at the tournament site. It was an eight court facility with hard courts. Mac had never played on a hard court but looked forward to trying something new. The Lynchburg Middle School courts were totally different from the tennis club she was used to in Charleston. There was no pro shop, a bare-bones bathroom facility and no wind screens. Fortunately, there was little wind but the background made tracking the ball difficult.

Mac's first round opponent was a talented 12-year-old local player who was playing up in the 14-and-under division. Mac spent the first set getting used to the court conditions, but eventually prevailed in a tough 3-hour match, 3-6, 6-4 and 6-2. Mac made use of her new drop shot with some success. There were no issues with line calls or scoring during the player-officiated match.

An hour later, Mac was back on court for her second round match. This time the match was chair-umpired and she was paired against the No. 2 seed. Mac's opponent was a nationally-ranked player and the best player Mac had ever played. Mac lost 6-1, 7-5, but improved considerably during the match. She made liberal use of her new-found drop shot and enjoyed moderate success, particularly as the match wore on. Her opponent was experienced and well-conditioned and moved forward well. Both players were all smiles after the match and hugged each other at the net. Since there was no feed-in consolation, Mac was eliminated from the tournament.

On the ride home Mac and Alice stopped at a McDonalds and enjoyed a Big Mac meal. This was a special treat for both since they seldom were near a McDonald's. The nearest McDonald's was in Buckhannon, an hour's drive from their home in Valley Head.

As Alice and Mac enjoyed their McDonald's meal, Mac excitedly talked about her tournament experience.

"That was really fun. I know I improved a lot from playing two really good players. When is the next tournament?"
"We'll be going to Ashland, KY in three weeks."
"That's great. It will give me some time to practice my serves and perfect the drop shot."

When Mac met Scott for her Thursday lesson, he again could not believe her improvement and after just two tournament matches. Because of her age, Scott knew that Mac's dream of winning Wimbledon was a long shot, but you could not deny her enthusiasm or athletic ability. Most female Grand Slam champions were playing world-class tennis when they were 14 or 15 and Mac was not close to world-class. Because of her exceptional talent, Scott did think she had a chance and he was going to do everything he could to give her that chance. Scott had been a D-1 college player and had 20 years' experience as a USPTA teaching professional. Scott discussed with Mac the path forward for improvement this way.

"Mac, because you are a great athlete, working out in the gym in an effort to become stronger and faster should not be necessary. You can stay fit by doing some regular stretching, yoga and light running. Improving your flexibility will be the key to avoiding serious injury as you play better competition.

Basketball in the winter and tennis in the summer should be sufficient for you to maintain your physical gifts. Even though you have been playing mostly right-handed, I think your abilities can be maximized by serving and receiving left-handed in the ad court and serving and receiving right-handed in the deuce court. I've seen you hit some great shots with either hand and this style of playing will make you a difficult opponent for top coaches to strategize against. I want you to be able to hit both left and right-handed overheads and hit drop shots with either hand. Volleys will be the most difficult, but I will show you the best grips to use and how to finish points at the net. In our lessons we will practice these skills until you have mastered them and can use them seamlessly in a match. Are you comfortable with the plan?"

"Yes, and I believe I can do it."
"I know you can. Do you have any questions?"
"Yes Mr. Flannigan, what about the string tension for my polyester string? I have been reading that the trend for professional players is lower tensions and most women professionals are playing with a string tension in the mid-forties. What tension do you think I should play with?"
"I would prefer you call me Scott and yes, you are correct about the current trend. I will have your racquets restrung at 45 pounds."

Little did Scott know that Mac had studied the life of the Brazilian star Gustavo Kuerten and how he had revolutionized professional tennis with his revolutionary use of *Luxilon Original* polyester string. "Guga" as he is affectionately known won the 1997, 2000 and 2001 French Open titles with a polyester string that was seldom used by professional players of that era. Mac even studied the physics behind the strings ability to produce more spin. A "snap back effect" occurs when the string gaps as the ball is struck and then snaps back into its original position once the ball leaves the racquet. This allowed professional players to hit with greater topspin than they could produce with conventional strings (gut or nylon). After Kuerten's triumphant runs at the French Open, most professionals gradually shifted to some variant of the polyester string. Some players even adopted a hybrid stringing with the mains strung with gut and the horizontals with poly.

The following week Mac was armed with two poly-strung racquets and was ready to play like a pro. However, it took some time to fully adjust to the feel of the string. Meanwhile, Scott was trying to get Mac to hit her ground strokes and serves harder (much harder). Everything in her lessons was more power and more topspin. Scott was teaching her the ATP forehand on all wide balls. Every opportunity to hit the ball hard was encouraged. When receiving serves, Mac was encouraged to use two hands on all balls served down the middle of the court. Scott even had a serving machine (Ace Attack) that could hit serves up to 130 mph and hit all the spins. It was the tennis version of a pitching machine in baseball. When working on service return, Mac would occasionally practice on an Ace Attack serving machine. Because the machine was expensive ($5,000+), Scott didn't use it often in lessons. The machine was available to club members for a $100 per hour rental fee.

Once Mac returned to Valley Head and started her practice sessions on her uncle's barn door, the sound of the ball hitting on the barn door gradually changed. It went from tap; tap; tap to thump; thump; thump. More power from Mac equaled more errant balls, but improvement did happen. Even Uncle Henry

71

noticed the sound change as he watched from his porch. The next week when Mac returned for her lesson, Scott was again impressed with her progress. He was starting to see Mac transform from a defensive retriever to an aggressive offensive player. Her mind set was changing from wait for my opponent to make errors, to force my opponent to make errors. After another lesson and a week of practice, Mac played another match with the male senior player who had beaten her 6-1, 6-2 a year earlier and this time she dominated with a 6-2, 6-2 thrashing. The same committee member who had initially voted to ban Mac from playing at the Club, did a total reversal and now was a total fan of Mac. He rightly recognized that Mac was not just a terrific player, but possessed an attitude and personality to match. After playing, Mac asked him about the drop shot.

"Could you show me how you hit your drop shot?"
"I would be happy to and will also show you how to defend it."

Thirty minutes later, Mac had learned the terms, redrop and angle drop and had practiced enough to gain a feel for both. After a week of practice and another lesson from Scott, Mac felt she was ready to use her newfound offensive skills and the drop shot in her next tournament in Ashland, KY.

The drive from Valley Head to Ashland was about 4 hours and Mac's first round match was scheduled for 10 a.m. Alice and Mac left Valley Head at 5:30 a.m. and easily made it to the tournament desk by 9:45. The Ashland Tennis Center was an impressive facility featuring 4 indoor and 11 outdoor hard courts (6 lighted), a practice wall, model clubhouse with locker rooms and a well-stocked pro shop. Mac's first round opponent was from TN and a nationally-ranked player whose ranking was not quite high enough to be seeded. Mac was happy to find out all matches would have chair umpires. As a result of car-lag (sluggishness from sitting long stretches in a car), Mac started a bit sloppy and dropped the first set, 6-4. She recouped and finally prevailed 4-6, 6-3, 6-1. In the third set, her serves and ground strokes were finding their mark and her hapless opponent was ultimately overwhelmed by Mac's power.

Meanwhile, Alice who had never been interested in sports, was gradually becoming more than just a casual spectator. She had always been interested in how tennis was affecting Mac emotionally, but until Mac started playing these out-of-state tournaments, Alice had shown little interest in the results. She was becoming more astute in her knowledge of the rules and more vocal in cheering for the winning shots that were fast becoming the hallmark of Mac's tennis.

Mac's second round opponent was the #4 seed, nationally ranked and the best 14-and-under player in KY. With Alice cheering every winning shot that came off her racquet, Mac was able to demolish her opponent 6-3, 6-3. Alice's vocal support invigorated Mac and was a big help in keeping Mac focused and in the moment. It was the best tournament match that Mac had ever played as Mac's left-handed opponent had trouble dealing with Mac's ambidextrous barrage of aggressive shot-making. After comforting her dispirited opponent at the net, Mac sought out Alice and hugged her in a long emotional embrace. It was difficult to tell who was the most excited. Calling her dad was the next order of business and Mac's description of the match was filled with detail. When Mac and Alice returned to the tournament desk, they were given a next day start time at 9 a.m. Alice and Mac then set out to find a motel for the evening. By Valley Head standards, Alice and Fred were not poor, but Alice was slowly discovering that the combination of lessons, travel, entry fees and lodging was expensive and Alice worried that they might not be able to afford continuing with a regular tournament schedule. They settled on a Motel 6, and soon after dinner were fast asleep.

A bright sunny day greeted Alice and Mac as they left the motel and headed toward the Tennis Center. Mac's opponent (Mary) arrived 10 minutes late but was not defaulted. After some introductions, Alice, both players and the umpire headed to their assigned court. There was some bleacher seating alongside court #1 and Alice was thankful that the morning sun was at her back. During the warm-up, Mac quickly recognized that Mary was not as skilled as the players she had faced the day before. Mary had gained the third round via default, and the 13-year-old was fortunate to have advanced to the third round. Mac got off to a quick start and outclassed her hapless opponent 6-1, 6-1 in less than an hour. After a quick hug at the conclusion, Mac was ready to shop for a new tennis dress. She was hoping that her mom would be amenable to buying her a new outfit.

"Mama, can we look at tennis outfits in the pro shop?"
"No honey, we don't have the money for a new outfit right now."
"Can we go in and look?"
"Ok, but we are not buying. The prices in that shop are outrageous."
"Can I try a couple on?"
"Ok, but remember, we are not buying you a new outfit."
"Thank you, Mama. I love you so much."
"I love you too honey. Let's go look."

Once inside the shop, Alice and Mac made quite the pair while shopping. They both were tall (5' 9") females with blue eyes, silky auburn hair and figures that would be the envy of models and men everywhere. Even though there was a 25 year age difference, they could easily be mistaken for twins. Alice had told Mac when she was seven that she was adopted, but that did nothing to weaken the bond between them. They were extremely close and their love for each other was enduring.

"Wow, I really like this one. The skirt and top fit me perfectly."
"They look very nice, but we can't afford to buy right now."
"Ok, it's great to look and see what's available."

Mac was back on court at 12 noon and her opponent was the #1 seed. To Mac, she appeared to have the physique of a professional player. During the warm-up, Mac sensed that this opponent was not only very good, but would be the best female player she had played to date. There were several D-1 coaches in the crowd that were there not to watch Mac, but to watch her opponent Sarah. She was from NC and was a top 10 nationally-ranked player. Mac started the match nervously, but soon was firing on all cylinders. As the match wore on, it was obvious that this was going to be a tug of war matching two great athletes. With her mom cheering wildly, Mac finally prevailed 7-6, 5-7, and 7-5 in a well-played 3 ½ hour match. After the two weary players hugged each other at the net, Alice was so excited when she embraced Mac, she could hardly contain herself.

"Honey, you played great. You were a model of good behavior and I am so proud of you."
Mac responded. "I need to call dad."

Amidst all the excitement and without thinking, Alice shouted. "Let's go buy that outfit."

As they both bolted toward the tennis shop, Mac momentarily forgot about calling her dad. She was more concerned that maybe the outfit had been sold. Several girls had shown a strong interest earlier in the same outfit. As Alice and Mac happily left the pro shop with their purchase, they were approached by a well-known Athletic Director (AD) who was impressed with everything she had seen concerning Mac. She introduced herself as Dr. Virginia Jensen and explained how riveting the match has been and how much she enjoyed it.

"I was so impressed with your play and the composure you displayed under extreme pressure."
"Thank you very much. It was a fun match."
"Mac, upon your graduation from high school, I am prepared to offer you a 4-year athletic scholarship to play tennis for one of the best D-1 college programs in the country. I believe we have the finest facilities, the best coaches and the top academic programs anywhere." Alice and Mac both thanked her for the offer and her generous compliments.

Alice and Mac were both stunned and needed some time to process what this could mean for Mac. On the way back to the motel, Alice's excitement was unrestrained, but Mac's enthusiasm was muted.

"Oh, honey, wasn't that offer wonderful?" I think the AD has given you an opportunity of a lifetime. Your dad and I have been saving so that you could attend WVU, but now, you have an opportunity to attend a prestigious university at no cost and a chance to play college tennis at the highest level. Wow!"

"It was very nice, but I want to play professional tennis and win Wimbledon. Attending a university can wait, but professional tennis may not."

"When we get home we'll discuss it with your dad and see what he thinks,"

"Ok, but right now, I'm hungry and thirsty at the same time."

The following day, Mac's semifinal match was scheduled at 9 a.m. against the #7 seed. Mac's tournament inexperience gave her the false notion that this would be an easier match than her last one, since this was #7 seed instead of #1. In the warm-up, Mac was fairly certain that she could win and advance to the final. The match started well enough for Mac, but midway through the first set, the points started to get longer and more problematic for Mac. Her opponent could hit with slice on both sides, and could also hit high topspin lobs that landed just inside the baseline. Her serve, although not terribly hard was generally hit right at Mac, which made it tricky to decide whether to play a two-handed backhand or a one-handed forehand. When Mac came to the net, she often encountered a high defensive lob that required a reliable overhead to consistently finish. Mac's overhead was a weakness and a work in progress during her weekly lessons. It was a style Mac had never encountered and she struggled. Mac gave it all she had, but it was not enough as she lost by a pedestrian score of 6-3, 6-3.

Barely able to hold back her tears, Mac embraced her mother and attempted to explain what happened.

"I'm sorry, Mom, I did the best I could but she had an unusual style and was a tough opponent to play against. She was a much steadier player than I assumed she might be, but I have to give her credit. She withstood everything I threw at her and was able to play with very few misses. She was the better player today and hopefully I can learn from this match."

On the way back to Valley Head, both Mac and Alice were excited, but for different reasons. Mac was excited because she had won 4 matches in a tournament for the first time and she had a new tennis outfit that she couldn't wait to show her dad. Alice was thrilled because her 14-year-old daughter had just been offered a 4-year athletic scholarship to one of the finest universities in the country. Alice was also pleased that her daughter was in such good spirits. They both couldn't wait to tell Fred.

Fred was there anxiously waiting for their arrival when Alice and Mac pulled into the driveway. He had just gotten off from work and was tired, but not too tired to hear every detail of their trip. He greeted Alice and Mac with kisses and hugs and didn't have to wait long until Mac sprinted off to her bedroom, while shouting. "Dad, wait until you see my new tennis outfit."

While waiting for Mac to model her skirt and top, Alice and Fred discussed how fortunate they were to have such a lovely and talented daughter. She was well liked by everyone while remaining humble and outgoing. She could light up a room with a single smile. Alice told Fred about Mac's scholarship offer and Fred seemed more excited than Alice. The cost of a college education was expensive and Fred wanted Mac to earn a college degree.

"Dad, what do you think?"
"Darling, it's beautiful." You will outshine all of your tournament competition."

"Do you really think so?"

"I know so"

Alice immediately chimed in. "Honey, you look simply gorgeous."

"I can't wait until my next lesson and show Scott."

"Don't you want to wait until your next tournament?"

"I would rather wear it next week, if it's okay."

"If you must, you can wear it."

"Thanks, mom, I can hardly wait."

"Honey, your dad and I are thrilled that you were offered a tennis scholarship. We both think that's wonderful."

Mac smiled but said nothing; she had her own plan to attend and pay for her college education.

Due to a logging accident near Webster Springs, Mac and Alice were late for her lesson the following week. Once there Mac had to go to the restroom. It gave Scott an opportunity to inquire about the tournament in Ashland.

"Do you think the tournament was a positive experience for Mac?"

"Oh, yes, she won four matches and played well. The first day she was a little sluggish, but after that she was her old self."

"Why do you think she was sluggish that first day?"

"I believe the car ride wore her out."

"You mean you didn't spend the night in Ashland before her first round match."

"No, in order to save money, we have always gotten up early and driven to the tournament site the day of her first match."

"Oh Alice, you don't want to do that. A 5-hour car ride will make it difficult for anyone to physically be anywhere near 100%. You should arrive at the tournament site the day before her first match in order to give Mac the best chance of being successful."

"But that would mean another night of lodging and additional expenses. Our family is not poor by Valley Head standards, but the expenses involved in continuing tournament tennis looks to be a financial burden for us."

"Let's talk about this next week and I'll see what I can work out."

Alice thought it best not to mention the scholarship offer, thinking that Mac may want to tell Scott. Soon Mac appeared in her new outfit and Scott's one-word reaction was: "Wow!"

During Mac's shortened lesson, Mac told Scott all about the match she lost and the style that her opponent played. Scott took it all in and they proceeded to practice everything that concerned Mac with a focus on overheads. After her lesson and a practice match with an up-and-coming male junior, Mac and Alice took a well-deserved lunch break. While enjoying a trout lunch, they noticed Scott talking with Jim Chapman, the senior player who had initially been skeptical of Mac's presence at the Club. Jim owned a Mercedes car dealership and he and his wife were well-known patrons of the arts. After a hushed conversation, they approached Mac and Alice and asked if they might join them. Jim began by asking Mac about her tournament matches and how she felt about continuing tournament play. Mac eagerly explained to Jim how much she enjoyed the experience and her efforts to improve.

"It's been great, Mr. Chapman, the experience has been everything I had hoped for and more. I've met some very nice people and now have several friends that are tennis players."

"That's great Mac. Do you still have aspirations to be a professional player?"
"Oh yes, exclaimed Mac. "More than ever."

As she continued to freely express herself, Mac's bright blue eyes could not hide her passion and ambition. Jim was so awestruck by Mac's determination and the steel in her words, he was sure that if this young girl couldn't make it as a professional tennis player, she would surely be a star at something. In Jim's mind, she was poised to be a celebrity already. Even Alice marveled at the passion in Mac's voice as she clearly stated her tennis goals. While expressing herself, Mac did not have to pretend to be kind and humble. Being a nice person was at the core of who she was and it was evident through every component of her sparkling personality. Even Scott was impressed with the eloquence she showed when describing her goals. Scott had not heard her talk very much, since in her lessons, he had done most of the talking.

Next week and after Mac's lesson, Scott pulled Alice aside and told her of a plan that he had worked out with Jim Chapman.

"Alice, Jim has offered to pay all of Mac's tennis expenses while she is playing the tournament circuit. He has no interest in a signed contract or a return on his investment. He merely wants to give Mac the best chance of achieving her tennis goals."
"Oh, Scott, that's so nice, but we could never take the money. My husband would never agree to be a charity case. We may have to cut corners here and there, but we can afford to play a few tournaments every summer."
"Let me warn you of something Alice. The number one thing that can undermine the development of a young tennis player

is having to worry about money and the sacrifices they imagine their parents are making."

"No, I'm sorry Scott. Fred would never allow it."

"I should also tell you that Jim thinks the world of Mac and thinks of her as his daughter. He and his wife have no children and he has taken a great interest in Mac's progress. He even told me that if you couldn't accept the money as a gift, then you could pay him back once Mac has earned enough money through endorsements and/or prize money. He believes that Mac has star potential and will eventually be an endorser's dream. Will you at least think about it and discuss it with Fred and Mac?"

Reluctantly, Alice responded: "Okay, I will speak with Fred and let you know something next week."

"Thanks Alice. I'll look forward to next week's lesson."

Next week and after much negotiation with Fred and Mac, an agreement was reached on the condition that Jim would be paid back every penny of his financial commitment. When Alice told Mac that Jim would be financing her tennis, Mac committed to keep track of her expenses and give Jim a monthly accounting. At about the same time Mac started an Instagram account and began posting about her tournament experiences. She quickly gained about 200 followers; most from the Valley Head area.

Her next tournament was in Richmond, VA and Fred and Mac arrived the day before the tournament started. Fred decided to splurge and checked into a Hilton, where a hot breakfast was free. After a good night's sleep and a hot breakfast, Mac was ready to go. Once at the tournament site, Mac was pleasantly surprised to learn that all matches would be played on clay

(Har-Tru) courts and chair umpired. The Westwood Club offered first class facilities with a large heated swimming pool, a top restaurant and pro shop. Her first round opponent was a local player from Richmond, about Mac's height and impeccably dressed. In the warm-up, Mac surmised that a tough match might be ahead. But Mac quickly outclassed her opponent and won 6-2, 6-2. After a brief, but sincere hug at the net, Mac was ready to play again. Her next match was scheduled at 2 p.m., so a light lunch would come first.

Over lunch, Fred was pleased at how well Mac had played. He had rarely seen her play and was totally impressed with Mac's performance. And he told her so.

"Darling, you were magnificent out there. I was fascinated by your play and the scoring. It was different than I imagined."
"Oh dad, you're just saying that to be nice."
"No, Mac, I meant what I said. You were great."
"I play the #4 seed next and this match should be much tougher."
"I'm sure you will play great regardless of who you play."

Mac turned out to be a poor prognosticator as she crushed the # 4 seed, 6-2, 6-1. Mac was comfortable on the Har-Tru courts and the pin-point accuracy and the power of her shots were way too much for her opponent. Mac's dad was mesmerized by the array of shots that Mac was able to produce. When she hugged her dad afterwards, he only had one word to say. "Wow."

Mac blazed through the rest of the tournament and won the finals 6-4, 6-4. After receiving her large silver tray, Mac was all smiles. Several spectators wanted selfies and young autograph seekers wanted her signature. It was the first time that Mac had been in the spotlight after a tournament and she and her father were on cloud 9. On the way back to Valley Head, Fred and Mac stopped for a nice dinner and Mac had to call her mother.

At her lesson the following week, Mac told Scott all about the tournament. During her lesson, Scott could sense a change in Mac's confidence. After the lesson, Scott suggested to Alice that they play their next tournament in Atlanta. Scott felt Mac was ready to take on the best in the South. Atlanta was a hotbed of tennis and Scott knew that this junior tournament drew the best players in USTA's largest division. Of course Mac was ready and willing, but Alice had some reservations. "It's a long drive to Atlanta and Fred will be going with Mac. I want to make sure he's okay with it."

Upon returning home and hearing the change of plans; Fred responded. "Sounds great. Let's go."

Fred and Mac left early and arrived in Atlanta about 3 p.m. They decided to visit the tournament site before checking into their hotel. The Bitsy Grant Tennis Center had 28 courts (13 clay) and was the largest tennis complex in GA and the finest that Mac had ever seen. They checked the draw and found out that Mac was seeded #7 in the girls 14s and scheduled for a 9 a.m. start time. Tournament officials, based on Mac's last tournament results, felt she deserved a seed. Fred and Mac then checked into the Atlanta Hilton, now Fred's favorite hotel. As Fred would often say. "What's not to like." After their free hot breakfast, Mac checked in at the tournament desk and learned that the entire tournament would be played on clay. With umpires for every match and the tournament held on her favorite surface, Mac was eager to test her skills against the best in the South.

Three days later, Mac was holding the winner's trophy and soon after called her mom. She had won every match in straight sets and never lost her serve. Atlanta's tennis aficionados raved about her tennis skills, athleticism and especially her demeanor. Mac was not only the best player in the tournament but surely gave the best interview. A sports reporter from the Atlanta Journal-Constitution, who had been watching the finals, was blown away by Mac's performance. As Mac left the awards ceremony, he hustled after her and asked for an interview. Mac, who had carefully watched Roger Federer's many post-match interviews, was well-prepared to answer any and all questions from the reporter.

"Mac, how do you feel about winning the tournament?"
"I'm obviously pleased, but none of that would have been possible without the support of the sponsors, tournament officials and some incredible opponents. I would also like to thank by parents and my coach in Charleston for giving me their unwavering support."
"Do you have any long-term goals in tennis?"
As Mac sparkling blue eyes carefully studied the reporter, she convincingly replied. "I hope to win Wimbledon one day."
The reporter appeared momentarily hypnotized and after a long pause, responded "I believe you will and thank you for the interview."

On the long ride home, Fred was still in shock with what he had witnessed. He was thinking to himself; maybe winning Wimbledon is a possibility. Since they had taken quite a few photos, Mac was thinking about her next Instagram posts. She ended up posting nine photos; one of each of her opponents, complete with first and last names. One photo of Fred and Mac holding the championship trophy and two pictures of the tennis facility.

At Mac's next lesson with Scott, Mac recounted her Atlanta experience. Mac had greatly exceeded Scott's expectations and he was elated with her results. But no one was more elated than Jim Chapman. Jim was so pleased that he could barely contain himself. "I knew you could do it. I just knew." Mac and Jim then played their weekly match and Jim barely avoided a double bagel. The score was 6-0, 6-1 and no one could know for sure if that one game might have been a gift. But Jim was sure that Mac's talent was undeniable and believed more than ever that the sky was the limit for Mac.

Chapter 13

The fall term at Mill Creek started the following week and after some ardent hugs, Mac said goodbye to Scott and Jim. She would be back in 9 months, but for now she would focus on her school work and basketball. In Valley Head tennis was no big deal, but girls' basketball was a big deal and the community around Mill Creek was expecting big things from their girls. Big things were expected from Mac academically when school administrators recommended to Mac's parents that she skip the 9th grade. Since Mac had scored so high on the ACT and the SAT, and Mac was by far the best student in school history, 10th grade AP classes and honor studies would better suit Mac's intellectual abilities. So Mac started the year as a 10th grader. Mac did miss the one-on-one competitive nature of tennis, but she now focused on basketball and playing a team game with her friends. Her teammates had been playing basketball all summer and once practice started, their improvement was obvious to Mac. Since the coaches felt this year could be record-breaking, practice sessions were more intense than in previous years. When the season started, Mac felt she was in the best shape of her life.

Their first game was at home and against powerhouse Elkins High. The Tygart Valley gymnasium was packed and the crowd was uncommonly noisy. Mac and the team got off to a fast start and the game stayed close until the final seconds. Mac was fouled with 3 seconds left and was on the foul line shooting a 1 and 1. The crowd was suddenly silent as Mac took her customary one dribble and a deep breath. Unexpectedly she missed the first shot and Tygart Valley lost by the final score of 65-64. Mac was devastated, but her teammates and coaches would not let her anguish override the team's effort against an excellent Elkins team. They knew that Mac was the key to a winning season and allowing Mac to stress over a missed foul shot was not an option.

The team finished the season with a won-lost record of 21-2 and good enough to qualify for the 8-team Class A State Finals held at the Charleston Civic Center. In the first round, they defeated Union 65-40 and in the second round defeated Tug Valley 60-55. The finals was played against defending State Champion Cameron High. Mac finished with 30 points, 15 assists and 14 rebounds, but it was not enough as Tygart Valley lost 72-65. Mac was named to the all-tournament team along with one of her teammates. A large crowd from the Mill Creek area followed the team to Charleston and left thinking about next year when all their starters would return.

Once the school year was over, Mac restarted her lessons and training at the Charleston Tennis Club. She had just turned 15 and would now have to play in 16-and-under events. Scott had big plans for Mac and laid out his vision for the summer schedule with Mac and Alice.

"Mac, you finished last summer great by winning two tournament titles, and you did well enough to qualify for the girls' 16s Nationals in San Diego, CA. The Barnes Tennis Center has 23 outdoor hard courts, so in order to get ready, we'll need to have our training sessions on hard courts. I believe your game is well-suited for the faster surfaces, so this transition should benefit you. The tournament will be held the first week in August, so we'll have plenty of time to prepare. You will need to fly from Charleston to San Diego and arrive two days early in order to adjust to the court surface and recover from jet lag. Do either of you have any questions?"
"Scott, do you think I'm ready for the Nationals?"
"Absolutely."
"It seems like it will be awfully expensive. Do you think Jim will be on board?"
"I've already talked with Jim and he thinks you are ready and the experience should be well-worth the expense."
"Okay Scott. Mom, what do you think?"
"Your mom can be a nervous wreck when it comes to flying, so Fred would need to take you. We will discuss it with him tomorrow."

As Mac's lesson began, Scott could see no apparent rust in her game. Mac had learned to hit the ball hard on both sides, so putting it all together would be the challenge. Experimenting with different string tensions and different racquets was a weekly endeavor. It was important that Mac was comfortable with her equipment. Scott had scheduled only three tournaments for Mac and the first one was The Charleston Women's Tennis Open held at the Charleston Tennis Club in June. There was $5000 purse for the singles only tournament and Scott felt the prize money should draw some top ex-college players and teaching pros from the tri-state area. Mac would enter as an amateur and would not be eligible for prize money.

The 3-day 64-draw tournament featured a variety of ex-college players plus some current college stars. It was a strong field and would offer Mac some strong competition. Mac entered the tournament unseeded and after winning her first two matches, played the #1 seed. She had been the number one player at West Virginia University (WVU) and was a recent graduate just starting her professional career. Mac was gracious in defeat and praised her opponent after the match.

"Mom, she was really good. I wish I could practice with her every day."
"You did fine honey, it looked like you had fun."
"I did and we exchanged phone numbers. She promised to text me and keep me informed of her professional progress."

Mac's next tournament was a hard court junior tournament in Columbus, Ohio. Mac breezed through the 16-and-under division without losing a set.

Mac and Scott then set about preparing for the National Girls' 16s in San Diego. Scott put an emphasis on serving and finishing at the net; particularly the overhead. Fred had agreed to take Mac to CA and it wasn't long before Mac and Fred were off to CA. Arriving two days early turned out to be a great idea and Mac had no trouble finding suitable practice partners. The National Girls' 18s was held in conjunction with the 16s and Mac felt fortunate to practice with the #1 seed in the Girls' 18s. Mac was practicing so much that Fred thought she might wear herself out, but Mac brimmed with energy after every practice session. After practices, Fred and Mac were both enjoying the amenities of the Hilton San Diego.

Mac's first round match was against the #4 seed, a Californian slated to attend Stanford in the fall on a full tennis scholarship. As the match began, Mac quickly realized that this girl was really good and she quickly settled in for a long hard-hitting match. In the stands and unnoticed by most, was John Donahoe, the CEO of Nike and Phil Knight, the company's founder. They had come to see the #4 seed and possibly offer her a shoe deal at the tournament's conclusion. Those plans went out the window when Mac prevailed in 3 tough sets and gave notice to the rest of the field that she was a contender. John met with Mac briefly after her match to offer his congratulations. To say that he was impressed with this young girl from WV would be an understatement of the highest order. Mac was gracious as always and thanked him for watching. John informed Mac that he looked forward to watching her future matches. Later, he had his staff research the background of this tennis prodigy from WV. After five more matches and two additional upsets, Mac advanced to the finals against the defending 16-and-under National Champion and the #1 seed. With a crowd of 1,000 engaged spectators, Mac won 7-5, 7-5 to claim the National Girls' 16s title. Fred was blown away by her play, but not as impressed as Nike's CEO, who after the match, offered Mac a 5-year 10 million dollar shoe deal. He was not only impressed with Mac's tennis, but with her looks, her presence and the charisma she exuded during and after all her matches. This teen's star power was evident for all to see and John knew that Mac was a marketer's dream. He had witnessed this radiant beauty win over a fascinated crowd and he knew that this might be only the beginning. Fred and Mac thanked the CEO profusely and said they would like some time to look over the contract. Mac had already called her mom after the match, but then had to call again after the Nike offer.

On the plane ride home Mac carefully read every word of the 12-page contract. She knew that her first endorsement check would be enough to repay Jim Chapman with interest. She had always worn Nike shoes, so there should be no issues with comfort or performance. She couldn't wait to tell Scott and Jim.

Once Mac and Fred were settled back in Valley Head, she started posting on her Instagram account. She posted a short video that Fred had taken showing Mac and her final's opponent sitting on a courtside bench actively laughing and giggling as though they were long-lost friends. To see these two former adversaries enjoying the moment was an incredible sight to witness. They both promised to stay in touch.

When Mac returned to Charleston for her next lesson, she was surprised to learn that Scott already knew about her tournament success. With Mac being the only West Virginian in the tournament, her results were big news for Charleston's largest newspaper, the Charleston Gazette. Numerous stories had been written about her progress. The Intermountain News, which covers news in Randolph County, WV had also been covering Mac's results. With the approval and urging of Jim's lawyers, Jim and Scott, Mac, Fred and Alice agreed to the terms of the Nike shoe deal. In order to fulfill the contract terms it would require a considerable time commitment from Mac, but all agreed that this would be a positive life-changing event for the entire family and Mac was excited to enter into a 5-year deal. Once the announcement was made by Nike, the story became big news and was widely covered by the national media. Mac's Instagram followers exploded and one week after Nike's announcement, Mac had 1.2 million followers. Mac made history by becoming the youngest tennis player to secure a major shoe deal. The 15-year-old had yet to win a professional tennis match, but the media didn't care; she was famous and rich.

Chapter 14

$\mathcal{B}$efore the fall term started, Mac and her parents were confronted with another decision suggested by Randolph County school officials. It was their recommendation that Mac skip another grade and go straight to the 12th grade. The 15-year-old would then have the option to take online college courses at WVU. Mac thought this was a great idea since she was anxious to take college courses and have subject matter choices. So Mac began the school year as a senior. She still was required to take some honor courses, but most of her classes were independent study. She had three Nike commitments during the school year and none conflicted with her basketball schedule. Her first obligation was a trip to New York City to meet and mingle with several prominent Nike shareholders. It was a formal cocktail party plus dinner at the famous Waldorf Astoria. Alice disregarded her nervousness about flying and agreed to accompany Mac to New York. Mac was scheduled to be one of the after dinner speakers and was given 5 minutes to say nice things about Nike. When the day finally arrived in early October, Mac and Alice were met at their home by a chauffeured limousine and taken to the Airport in Charleston. During the flight, Mac prepared her presentation while Alice napped. They flew first-class to New York and then were ushered into one of the hotel's finest suites. During the cocktail party, Mac and Alice were easily the stars of the event. Alice was not much for small talk, so she let Mac control much of the conversation. Alice and Mac spent some time with John and Phil Knight, who were spell-bound by both Alice and Mac. They found it so improbable that these two beautiful and poised women could emerge out of a small town in the hills of WV.

After dinner and a nice introduction by John, Mac was ready for her time in the spotlight. Mac and Alice had both bought formal gowns in Charleston for the occasion. Mac wore a red halter neck gown which had a band encircling the neckline connected to a sleeveless bodice which left the shoulder and part of the back bare. It was slightly daring for a teenager, but tasteful for the occasion. Alice wore a gold bias cut gown that accentuated her body perfectly. Her curves were on display and with her long auburn hair, gave her a sophisticated but regal look. Mac retained her signature pony tail and both wore half-carat diamond stud earrings. Three-inch heels complemented their look.

An erect Mac stood before the small dinner crowd and slowly gazed around the room. There was total silence as people studied this radiant young beauty from WV. Even the waiters stood still. With her hands clasped in front of her and without notes, Mac began: "Mr. Donahoe, Mr. Knight, thank you for giving me the opportunity to represent Nike. My first pair of sneakers were Nikes and from that moment I have always worn Nike shoes. In addition to adding comfort to our lives, sneakers express our individuality and make statements about who we are. I've known it to be a great brand run by great people and I am happy to be a part of the Nike tradition." After another pause, Mac continued: "I would also like to recognize my favorite person in the whole world, my mom. I love her so much. Stand up mom." As a surprised Alice slowly rose amidst a polite applause, Mac's dazzling smile permeated the room. She concluded her presentation this way: "In conclusion, I want to thank God for giving me the ability to pursue my dreams. Thank you so much." Because the crowd was so smitten with this articulate teen, very few attendees heard the bulk of Mac's speech. She had won them over in the first 30 seconds and after she finished, she was given a rousing round of applause. John and Phil now knew that Mac was not only special, but Nike had hit the promotional jackpot. In the future, Mac would be given many opportunities to shine.

At the conclusion of all speeches, most of the crowd gathered around Mac and Alice. Some were hoping that Mac's shine might rub off. Others wanted selfies and a few young waiters wanted autographs. Mac and Alice patiently fulfilled all reasonable requests and seemed to enjoy the attention. Over in one corner, John and Phil discussed Mac's impact. They weren't used to being alone at the conclusion of these events and were dumbfounded by Mac's popularity.

On the plane ride back to Charleston, Alice was still reliving the previous day's events, while Mac was content to work on her honors project.

Once back in Valley Head, Mac and Alice informed Fred of every detail of their New York trip. Fred, being a great listener, was happy to hear of their experiences. He even wanted Mac to repeat her 5-minute talk. After some gentle urging from Alice, Mac acquiesced. They continued to talk well into the night and even new outfits for church became a topic of discussion. Mac and Alice decided a Saturday trip to Clarksburg would be an ideal time to shop for new outfits for church. They even agreed to buy Fred a new sports coat.

The next morning Mac and Alice were off to the Meadowbrook Mall near Clarksburg. They decided to take the scenic route touching Monongahela National Forest. The drive would take about an hour and 45 minutes, but it was one of the most beautiful drives in West Virginia and they were in no hurry. The mall was a large indoor mall with over a hundred stores, restaurants and spa. Considered one of the top three malls in WV, Meadowbrook Mall was a shopper's dream. After a morning of shopping and a stop to have their nails done, Mac and Alice took a lunch break at Chick-fil-A and mapped out the afternoon's shopping. They both wore Mac's signature Nike sneakers with a single word Mac on the heel. They searched the aisles of stores like American Eagle, Dick's Sporting Goods, Target, Ulta Beauty and Victoria Secret. By late-afternoon they were able to find a nice sport coat for Fred and church outfits for Mac and Alice. As they left the mall, a stranger grabbed for Alice's purse. Mac dropped her packages and in one quick motion grabbed the stranger's arm while giving him a swift kick to the groin. As the purse snatcher lay curled up in the fetal position, Alice called 911, while Mac hovered over the thief. Soon the police arrived and the purse-snatcher was arrested. Alice was shaken up, but Mac took the incident in stride. She was a person of action and no one was going to harm her mom while she was around. Mac called Fred to let him know what had happened and assured him that Alice was a little shaken but okay. Soon they headed home.

Even after her tournament successes, the Nike shoe deal and all the accolades that followed, Mac was eager to begin the basketball season. She had been able to get free Nike basketball shoes for the entire team and Mac and her teammates were eager to pursue a State Championship. The season began with a road trip to Elkins and a rematch with powerhouse Elkins High. This time Mac and her teammates won a hard-fought contest, 64-60. The partisan crowd was dumbstruck, since losing to Tygart Valley had never before happened. The mood was festive on the bus ride back to Mill Creek. However, what might have been an undefeated season was ruined when the following week, most of the team, including Mac were sidelined with bad cases of flu. They were forced to default two games due to a lack of players. They did finish the season with an excellent won-lost record of 20-2, which was good enough to qualify for a spot in the Class A State tournament finals. Held at the Charleston Civic, this time Mac and her teammates were not to be denied; they swept through the tournament defeating defending champion Cameron High 70-56 in the final. Mac was selected the tournament's most valuable player (MVP) and she and a teammate were named to the all-state first team.

The following day, classes at Tygart Valley High were cancelled and the town of Mill Creek held a parade in the team's honor. Trucks were decorated in the school's colors and the High School band played their rendition of "We are the Champions". The team walked in front of the band waving wildly to the crowd which lined Main Street. The throng of roughly 500 cheered loudly amid scattered chants of Macken ZEEE, Macken ZEEE. To the delight of Alice and Fred, scholarship offers to play college basketball, skyrocketed for Mac's services. However, Mac was not impressed as she was ready for some tennis. Mac concluded her senior year by graduating with multiple honors and chosen as the class valedictorian. In her speech, and after thanking everyone in sight, she encouraged her fellow graduates to be kind to one another and to pursue their dreams.

Tennis couldn't begin soon enough for Mac and when the time came for her first lesson, she was anxious to start. She greeted Scott with a warm hug and bounded onto the teaching court ready to hit tennis balls. Scott was also eager, but not to hit balls, but to explain to Mac his plan for the summer.

"Mac, last year you had a great summer and I think you're ready for the next step. I think your goal for the summer should be to qualify for the US Open in New York. It's the last Slam of the season and I think you're ready."
"You really think I'm ready for professional tennis?"
"Yes, I know you are. But the first step is to qualify. The winner of the National Girls'18s in San Diego qualifies for a spot in the main draw at the Open."
"But I've never played any professional players before, not even in practice."
"That's okay, there is a first time for everything and this is your time."
Mac's blue eyes twinkled as she said: "Okay, what's the plan?"
"The plan is to play two hard court tournaments to prepare for San Diego. The first one will be a small prize money tournament in Atlanta for professional women. You will probably have to play the qualifying. The second tournament

will be another prize money event in Cincinnati. And then on to San Diego. What do you think?"

"I trust you Scott. If you think I'm ready, I'll do my best."

"I know you will and it should be good enough."

For the rest of summer, Mac played only on hard courts, playing against the best competition the Club could offer. She always found time to play with Jim Chapman, who was her biggest supporter at the Club. Instead of playing sets, they would just hit for an hour. A hitting session with Mac could be exhausting, especially for a senior. But Jim enjoyed their sessions immensely. He liked being around Mac and besides, he was preparing for Senior Nationals.

Alice accompanied Mac to Atlanta for her first tournament of the summer and they arrived two days before the qualifying began. In order to qualify for the main draw, Mac would have to win two matches. Her first match was against a teaching pro from Atlanta who had been a tour player when she was younger. The match was not umpired, but the teaching pro was quite fair and the match concluded with no line-calling issues. Mac played well in winning 6-4, 6-3. Afterward, her gracious opponent was profuse in her praise of Mac's ambidextrous style. She also told Mac that she was the best woman athlete she had ever played. Those comments meant a lot to Mac, since this teaching pro was a former tour player and knew well the competition.

"Do you have any advice that would help me improve?"

"The tour can be a tough grind; you have to love what you're doing. I think you love playing tennis, but you have to embrace the travel and meeting new people. You must relish taking care of your body. Eat right and sleep right and you can be successful. The margin of error in pro tennis is slim and the difference between winning and losing can boil down to just a couple of points, so focus on the present and forget past mistakes."

"Thanks a lot, I will remember that advice and I will remember you."

"Thanks Mac and good luck on the tour."

Mac's second match was late in the day and against a junior player from Florida. Mac noted that she had sculptured legs and a great tan. Again there was no umpire and Mac recognized early in the warm up that this Florida girl was really good. As the match wore on, bad line calls started to affect the momentum of the match. It brought back memories of her 12-and-under match years earlier, but Mac was not about to repeat the mistakes of the past. After a critical line call in the first set tie-breaker, Mac began to drop shot at every opportunity. At first it was only slightly effective, but as the match wore on, this girl started to tire. Mac's quickness started turning the match. At the end, the Florida girl had quit running for drop shots and Mac won 6-7, 6-4 and 6-1.

The next day Mac was in the main draw of the $10,000 tournament and her match was chair umpired. She drew the #2 seed, a professional player from the Czech Republic. She was a strong mature woman with a WTA ranking of 160. Mac eventually lost a hard-hitting match 6-3, 6-3.

Mac was disappointed, but realized that this was a great experience and a needed stepping stone toward her goal. She explained to her mom the match result this way.

"Mom, that woman was really good, but I felt the match was closer than the score indicated. I know the shots I need to work on in order to play at that level. I'm anxious to go over the match with Scott when we get back to WV."

"I thought you played great honey and I'm sorry you lost. You played some super points."

"We did have some great points and it's never fun to lose, but I enjoyed the match. The journey is the most important thing. I wish I could practice with her every day."

The following week, Mac gave Scott an analysis of her first round loss. She told Scott the situations where she made errors and what shots she needed to work on. That was all Scott needed to hear and that's where the lesson started. Scott was pleased that Mac had make it through the qualifying.

Cincinnati was her next pro tournament with $20,000 in prize money and more quality players. Even though there were no top 50 players, the top eight seeds were all ranked in WTA top 100. Mac again had to play the qualifying and lost in her second qualifying match against a former NCAA Champion. Even though she lost in the last round of the qualies, she got in the main draw as a 'lucky loser' when the number 8 seed had to withdraw because of illness. Mac knew that she was lucky to still be in the tournament and was intent on making the most of it. In her main draw first round match, she blasted away with a nonstop barrage of offensive tennis, and it was good enough to upset the #7 seed 4-6, 6-4 and 6-4. When Mac came off the court, she embraced her mom and whispered.

"Mom, that was the best I have ever played. All the shots Scott and I have been practicing were landing inside the lines."

"I was rooting for you as hard as I could and you were simply amazing."

Mac won two more rounds in the main draw before losing to the #1 seed in the quarterfinals, 6-2 and 6-3. Coming off the court, the first words out of Mac's mouth were: "I believe I'm ready for the next tournament?"

After three days of focused practice in Charleston, it was off to the National Girls' 18s in San Diego. Mac and Alice arrived two days early and discovered to Mac's surprise that she was the #7 seed. The seeding committee had been favorably impressed with her win in last year's Girls' 16s final. After considerable practice on the hard courts of the Barnes Tennis Center, Mac felt ready to give it her all. The 128 main draw event was a week-long affair. To win the tournament and qualify for a spot in the US Open would require winning 7 matches.

Her first match was against an overmatched 17-year-old and was over in less than an hour. As Mac continued to sail through the draw, she began to realize that the professional events she had played previously had prepared her nicely for this particular tournament. Mac's composure and charisma had made her a crowd favorite and she did not disappoint. She breezed through the draw until the finals where she was paired against last year's finalist and the #1 seed. In the warm-up Mac sensed that this girl played more like the professionals she had played earlier in the summer. With the crowd behind her, Mac won a hard-hitting match 7-5, 4-6 and 6-3. She was bound for New York to play in the world's biggest tennis event; The US Open.

After the finals, Alice could barely contain her excitement. She hugged Mac, called Fred and recorded the trophy presentation. The crowd gave both players a standing ovation, but saved the loudest response for Mac's acceptance speech. She had endeared those in attendance which included Nike's John Donahoe and Phil Knight. John and Phil were high-fiving each other like they were 10-year-old kids. Mac was exceeding their expectations and her enthusiasm and bubbling nature were contagious. Mac was equally good in front of the camera or microphone and the following day her Instagram followers soared.

Chapter 15

When Scott, Fred, and Jim found out the news, they were of course initially overjoyed, but soon started planning their trip to New York. They knew they would have access to great seats, since Mac would be given free tickets to her player's box. As soon as Mac arrived back in Charleston, Scott revealed his plans to Mac and Alice for Mac's Open preparation.

"Mac had a tremendous result in California and now has the opportunity to display her considerable talent to the tennis community in New York. The effort Mac has made to improve her tennis has brought her to this stage in her tennis career. In order for Mac to be at her best in New York, I think a 3-week training block on hard courts would be the best preparation. I have arranged with Jim Chapman a bedroom in his house for

Mac during her 3-week stay. I have also begun to arrange some excellent hitting partners for Mac. One of the players is an experienced top 50 professional from Belarus, named Anastasia. I will house her and her coach during their stay. There will be no charge for the experience and Mac can have use of the Club facilities for the entire training session. After a week's break, Mac should be ready for New York. What do you think?"

"Scott, this has happened so fast. What do you think honey?"

"Mom, it seems like a wonderful opportunity and I'm ready to do it. You and dad could periodically visit during my training."

"It sounds like a super plan, but let me run this by your dad and make sure he's okay with it. Scott, we will let you know tomorrow."

After a quick okay by Fred, Mac embarked on what was to be a successful training block. Mac and Anastasia became close friends and Mac helped her with English and the Belarusian helped Mac with Russian. They decided to play doubles together at the US Open. After a short break, Mac, Alice and Fred were off to New York. Fred reserved a two-bedroom suite at the New York Hilton and even though it was not one of the two official tournament hotels, the Hilton was Fred's favorite.

Once settled in their hotel, unforeseen surprises awaited. The first was the Cadillac service provided by the tournament for travel to and from the US Open site. Three days before the start of the tournament, Mac and her parents were chauffeured to Arthur Ashe Stadium and the player's entrance. Above the double-door entrance Mac studied Arthur Ashe's famous quote: "Start where you are. Use what you have. Do what you can." As they entered the first of three floors, they approached a hectic hub of activity called Player Operations. It's where coaches and players schedule practice court time. Mac was hoping to see Anastasia there, but no luck. After scheduling some practice time for the afternoon, they toured the player's locker rooms, which were adjacent to an area for pre-match warm-ups. It was complete with exercise bikes, TV screens, a stringing area and a drop-off for laundry. The first floor also included one of Mac's favorites, the Nordstrom Gifting Suite. Main draw players were given a $1,600 credit to buy anything from player-only apparel to Tiffany tennis bracelets. The first floor also housed the Player's Café, which contained sandwiches, pasta and healthy snacks. The second level featured a large lounge and the main player cafeteria. The lounge had a juice bar which overlooked the practice courts. Each player had a $125 meal credit that they could use in the juice bar, cafeteria or the downstairs café. Mac then toured the third floor which had a complete gym, semi-private physio training beds and a complimentary hair salon. Mac was surprised by the facilities, but Mac's parents were dumbstruck. They couldn't believe their little girl had become a tennis celebrity. They decided to have lunch in the second floor cafeteria.

After an intense afternoon practice session, Mac, Scott and her parents relaxed at the juice bar where everyone enjoyed a fresh juice drink. Mac's smooth skin was still glistening with perspiration, when Alice whispered to Mac.
"I believe that blond guy over there is staring at you."
"I don't think so mom, but he is cute."
"Honey, he may be cute but he's too old for you."
Moments later, a tall blond young man walked over to Mac and said: "Are you Mac, the gifted player from West Virginia?"

"Yes, I'm from West Virginia and my name is MacKenzie, but my friends call me Mac."

"It's nice to meet you Mackenzie. My name is Brian and would you like to play mixed doubles with me?"

A startled Mac shot a quick glance toward a nodding Scott and replied: "I would love to."

"Would you like to practice with me tomorrow morning?"

"Yes, if it's okay with my coach."

Scott responded, "I think that would be great. If a 9 a.m. practice time is agreeable, I will arrange a court time."

"Okay, I will see you tomorrow."

Scott informed Mac that Brian was the #3 ranked American and seeded #31 in the men's singles.

"Do you think three events is too many for me?"

"No", replied Scott. "The experience will be good for you."

The foursome had decided earlier than Mac would declare herself a professional for the US Open and make herself eligible for prize money. She could then, as a 17-year-old become part of the WTA tour. Additionally, first round losers in the singles would receive $81,500 dollars. Mac really didn't care much about the money, but was focused on improving, so if declaring as a professional and playing three events would help her improve, she was all in.

The next morning, Mac and Scott met Brian and his coach and they proceeded to have a great practice session. Mac had never hit with a male player as good as Brian and he had never hit with a young woman as beautiful as Mac. After finishing their practice, Scott and Brian's coach discussed equipment and strategies, while Mac chatted with Brian. Brian was transfixed with the intelligence and bubbly personality of

Mac. He couldn't believe someone so young could have developed the wit and looks that continuously flowed from Mac. He was sure that she was a star in the making. Unfortunately for him, he was 22 years old and had a serious girlfriend. Otherwise, a younger Brian would have jumped at the chance to date Mac. Instead he launched into a strategy session with Mac.

"MacKenzie, are you agreeable to playing the ad court? I've always played the deuce side and am not as comfortable returning in the ad court in doubles."
"Brian, you can call me Mac and yes I am okay with serving and receiving on the ad side."
"Are you okay with the I-formation and me poaching when you're serving?
"I haven't really played doubles before, but I will try to adjust to anything you suggest."
"That will be great Mac and maybe we can practice again before our first match."
"I will look forward to that."

As Brian left for a session in the gym, he reflected on his positive interaction with Mac. Most beautiful women Brian had met were stuck-up divas and Mac was certainly not that.

After a couple of back and forth texts, Mac finally met up with Anastasia and they had a spirited practice with both coaches on court. Anastasia was surprised at Mac's improvement and her command of the Russian language. Mac was not one to leave anything started unfinished, so in the last couple of weeks, she had completed two online courses in Russian. Mac's command was so good, that they conversed mostly in Russian. It was quite a sight seeing two young women, one

American and one Russian, laughing and talking in Russian. You might have guessed they were sisters, and that world peace was right around the corner. Mac discovered that Anastasia preferred playing the ad court, which was fine with Mac, since she would gain experience in playing the ad side with Brian and the deuce side with Anastasia.

After another practice sessions with Anastasia and one with Brian, it was time for Mac to make her first Slam singles appearance. She was scheduled to play an American from California in Louis Armstrong stadium. The Stadium held approximately 14,000 spectators and it was packed. As the players were introduced, each were given a polite round of applause. Mac's opponent was a former NCAA Singles Champion and the number 27 seed. Mac got off to a slow start and lost the first set 6-1. The crowd, who expected a close match, was mostly silent during the first set and many left to watch a men's match on Arthur Ashe Stadium. Those that stayed would get the tennis show of their life when Mac's powerful ground strokes started finding their mark. The remaining 7,000 spectators started pulling for Mac to make a comeback and Mac did not disappoint. With a delirious crowd cheering loudly for every winner that came off her racquet, Mac would win the final two sets 6-4 and 6-2. Not only did Mac win the match, she won over the crowd. During her on court interview afterwards, a jubilant Mac further endeared the crowd by her thoughtful remarks; both thanking the crowd and complimenting her opponent's play. On her way out of the stadium, people clamored for autographs and selfies and Mac did her best to satisfy everyone. Finally, security had to escort her out of the stadium. In the interview room following her match, reporters clamored for a seat and by the time Mac arrived, it was standing room only. Mac was big news and reporters wanted some answers. A New York Times reporter led off the questioning.

"Everyone wants to know how a teenager from the hills of West Virginia with no tennis courts within 100 miles was able to pull off an upset like you did today."
"No one plays tennis at this level without the love and support of family. I also want to thank my coach Scott for his guidance, my friend and mentor Jim Chapman, my friends in the Mill Creek area and today's crowd. I know I could not have played as well without the enthusiasm of the crowd."
"But your athleticism and talent are undeniable. To whom do you attribute these immense gifts?"
"I was blessed by God for any gifts that I have and I just try to use those gifts to the best of my ability."
"Do you think you can win the US Open?"
Mac flashed her signature smile and replied "I don't think much about winning tournaments, but focus only on my next match."

Thirty minutes later Scott came in and rescued Mac by telling reporters that she had to get ready for her doubles. No one asked about her obvious beauty or whether she had a boyfriend. That would come later.

That evening Mac would celebrate with her parents, Scott, Jim Chapman, Anastasia and her coach. Anastasia had defeated a qualifier to win her first round match and all were in good spirits. Mac, Anastasia and her coach spent most of the evening laughing and conversing in Russian to the amusement of everyone at the table. Since all were having such a good time, there was no need for anyone to know what Mac and Anastasia were saying. They both were looking forward to playing doubles. Anastasia was unseeded in the singles and was thrilled to have made it into the second round. Both had the following day off from tournament play, but their coaches had scheduled a practice time in the afternoon. Once Mac and Anastasia began their practice, Mac became serious and the laughter stopped. She knew there was a time to fool around and a time for improvement and she was not one to waste practice time.

The next day Mac was scheduled for an evening match in Arthur Ashe Stadium. It was a rainy evening and the roof on the Stadium was closed. Mac seldom played under lights and took some time to adjust. Her opponent was a seeded player from Romania and the stadium was full with an estimated crowd of just under 24,000. Ashe was the largest tennis stadium in the world and 9,000 more than the next largest Grand Slam venue. The crowd quickly got behind the American but witnessed an up and down match. Although Mac was familiar with most of the rules, the bathroom breaks, the stalling, the medical time outs and arguments with the umpire were all new to Mac and affected her concentration. Despite the constant urging from the crowd and from her player's box, Mac lost a close match 4-6, 6-3, and 7-5. After hugging her opponent, Mac seemed disappointed, but not discouraged. Mac easily won over the crowd and was mobbed by souvenir seekers. When Mac was finally able to greet her mom afterwards, she was surprised by her mother's tears.

"What's wrong mom? You're crying."
"I'm so sorry you lost. I know you must be miserable. I was cheering for you as hard as I could, but I couldn't believe the number of bathroom breaks that girl took. She must have the bladder of a 3-year-old."

"It's okay. I'm not miserable; disappointed maybe, but not discouraged. I will learn from this experience and be ready the next time. That girl was good, but beatable."
"Oh, honey, you are such an angel. I love you so much."
"I love you too mom."

Earlier in the day, before the rain started, Anastasia had lost to a seeded player on one of the outdoor courts. The next day Mac was scheduled to play women's doubles and mixed doubles. Scott and Jim both left for Charleston after Mac's singles exit. So Mac's entourage now consisted of Alice and Fred.

The following day Mac and Anastasia were scheduled for a morning match outdoors. Before, during and after the match their chemistry was remarkable. Both had great fun; spoke Russian on the change-overs and thoroughly enjoyed themselves. Beating the number 3 seeds was icing on the cake.

In the afternoon, Mac and Brian easily won against an unseeded team. Even though they lost in the next round, Brian was utterly surprised at how well Mac played.

In the women's doubles, Mac and Anastasia went all the way to the finals, where they upset the defending champions to win their first Grand Slam title. Mac and Anastasia had a chemistry that was undeniable and they celebrated with hugs after every match. A record attendance for a women's doubles final was set in Ashe and the TV audience was also a record. The crowd thoroughly enjoyed every winning shot. For someone who had never played doubles, Mac's play bordered on the absurd. In eight doubles matches, Mac never lost her serve. Because of

Mac's success in the doubles, Alice and Fred opted to stay the full two weeks and enjoy the experience with their daughter. Mac pocketed just under $500,000 in prize money and her popularity increased with every match she played. During the women's doubles final, and as Mac was ready to serve, a male admirer shouted:

"Mac, will you marry me?"

Mac responded with a slight smile and then proceeded to serve an ace. Her beauty, poise and charisma endeared her to the New York fans and to several potential sponsors.

On the way back to WV, Alice showed Mac a contract that Wilson had offered Mac to exclusively play with their racquets. It was an endorsement deal similar to her Nike deal; ten million dollars over five years. Included was a million dollar signing bonus. Mac had always played with Wilson racquets so on the surface this seemed like a no-brainer. Mac carefully studied the contract on the plane ride home.

"Mom, this is a great contract. Even better than the Nike deal." There are very few time commitments. I will just have to play with Wilson racquets, have a W stenciled on my strings and use Wilson racquet bags. There's no reason that we shouldn't do it."
"Honey, it's a nice agreement and a lot of money, but maybe we should let Jim's lawyers look at it just to make sure."
"Okay mom, that's a good idea."

Once back home in Valley Head, Mac received a text from Scott congratulating her on her Grand Slam doubles title. A second text wanted to arrange a luncheon meeting with Mac and her parents at the Charleston Tennis Club to discuss plans for the future.

"Mom, I know that Scott wants to plan for the Australian Open next year and I've decided that whatever plan he has will not be the right one for me. I want to stay home and celebrate the holidays with my friends. I've been away from home so much that now it's time to relax and enjoy the holidays. We haven't even been to church for months and to spend Christmas and New Year's traveling to Australia doesn't seem right."
"Honey, that's fine with me. Australia is a long trip and staying home for the holidays sounds perfect."

The following week, Mac and her parents met Scott for lunch and Scott proceeded to lay out his goals for the coming year. "Thank you for meeting I would like…"

Before Scott could say anything further, Mac interrupted and said:

"Scott, your advice and planning have been invaluable and before you continue, let me say that I have no desire to play the Australian Open. I would rather spend time with friends and enjoy the holidays. My tennis dreams can wait."

Scott was struck with the conviction in Mac's words.

"I couldn't agree with you more, Mac. What I was about to reveal may surprise you; I will be leaving the Charleston Tennis Club at year's end to pursue my own dream. I plan to build the Scott Flanagan Tennis Academy near the airport which will have indoor and outdoor courts; both hard and clay. With financing help from Jim Chapman, we will build an apartment complex to house players and their families who wish to attend the academy full time. There is an excellent public school nearby and virtual learning will also be available. I want you to know that you will always be welcome at the Academy."

"Wow. That was a surprise."

"As I have said before, with a wife and three young children, traveling with you as a full-time coach is something that I cannot do. I hope you understand. My dream is here in Charleston."

"Can I still call or text you for advice?"

"Of course Mac, anytime you like."

After Scott left to teach his afternoon clinic, Mac and her parents lingered at their table to discuss Scott's plans. Mac began the conversation.

"I think it's great that Scott has a plan for his future and I think we need a plan for ours. Things have happened so fast, I haven't had much time to think about what lies ahead. I know I have made some money in tennis and I feel I can make some more. But the money is not important unless it can be used to help people in need and maybe at the same time achieve our dreams. Mom, Dad, what plans do you have?"

Fred answered. "The only thing we've done is to open a savings and checking account in your name at Mountain Valley Bank in Mill Creek, where your tennis earnings will be waiting for your decision on how to use them."

"I would like to give some money to the Randolph County Humane Society in memory of Daisy. They run a rescue shelter for dogs and puppies and could sure use the money. An orphanage in Wheeling always needs financial help and maybe a child could be as lucky as I've been and be blessed with loving parents."

"Fred and I do love you so much and we are the lucky ones; to have such a wonderful daughter."

Fred immediately chimed in. "Amen to that."

Mac continued. "I've also been thinking about our future tennis plans. My dream is still to win Wimbledon. The sponsorships and prize money are great, but I think we should give some money to those in need, before we spend it on ourselves. At church Sunday, I will ask the Lord for some guidance and then we can talk some more. Will that be okay, Mom?"

"Darling, I think that is a wonderful plan and Fred and I will also ask for the Lord's counsel. We know that we are blessed to have you as our daughter. We want you to know that your dream is our dream and we will do everything we can to help you."

After Sunday's church service, Mac and her parents gathered around the dinner table for a serious discussion about their future. Mac began by saying.

"I have some big ideas and I'm sure we will eventually have the financial resources to achieve them. I feel the rescue shelter, the orphanage and our church should receive donations first. Right now the church needs a new roof and an additional class room. After that, our house is almost 30 years old and needs remodeling; a new roof; new appliances and new furniture. Finally, to help me achieve my dream, I would like to build three tennis courts, one hard and one clay and one indoor. The clay court would be surfaced with red brick dust; just like the courts at the French Open. A two-bedroom cabin to house practice partners would complete my list.

"Darling that is quite a list. Is it doable Fred?"

"It's not only doable but an excellent list and well thought out. The three donations we can do right away. Next week, I will call a contractor friend of mine and get started on the house and the tennis courts. We have three acres of adjacent land that can be used for the courts and cabin."

Mac continued. "I've also decided that the best path for me is to play just five tournaments next year. I would like to play Indian Wells, Miami, the French Open, Wimbledon and the US Open. I only want to play combined tournaments where the men and women have equal prize money. My WTA ranking is 152 and I'm okay with qualifying if I have to. Anastasia and I have decided to play doubles in all five events. I know that most top players play warm-up tournaments leading up to the majors and some give half-hearted efforts in preparation. I've never given a half-hearted effort and don't want to start. I will do some training before the French Open on our clay court, if it's available. If not, I will train at Scott's Academy. I know dad needs to stay here and work with the brothers in auto repair. Mom, will you be available to go with me?"

"Absolutely, if it's okay with Fred."

"It is more than okay. I may even show up occasionally to watch Mac hoist the winner's trophy."

Fred and his contractor friend began the construction projects in October and were mostly finished by January 1st. The signing bonus from Wilson sped along the construction process. Mac enjoyed the holiday season with her friends and Fred put together a fireworks display to welcome in the New Year. The family plans were being executed to perfection and everyone was looking forward to the start of the New Year.

Chapter 16

All of the family plans for the New Year were unfolding beautifully as Mac began her preparation for BNP Paribus Open. Neither Mac nor Alice had ever been to Palm Springs and were looking forward to visiting Indian Wells. Mac purchased a ball machine for practicing on her new outdoor courts. Fred installed underground watering for the clay courts and a post-tension concrete foundation for the hard court. The hard court foundation was guaranteed not to crack. Once a week Mac and Alice would travel to the Charleston Tennis Club to practice with some of the area's top men players. She would always make sure to schedule an enjoyable practice session with Jim Chapman. Since Mac had been awarded a lifetime membership at the Club, lunch with Alice on the veranda was a welcome pause in the day's activities. With a greater understanding of tennis, Alice enjoyed watching many of Mac's practice sessions and continued to marvel at her talent and progress. Often they would find time to do some shopping at the local mall. They were quite a pair as they browsed the aisles of Charleston's best stores. Men of all ages would often gawk at the stunning pair. Mac barely noticed, but it made Alice uncomfortable and would sometime spoil their shopping experience.

As Mac continued her preparation in Valley Head, she immediately fell in love with her two outdoor courts. Fred had arranged for a retired military vet to do regular court maintenance. He would brush and roll the clay court daily and then brush the lines so that the court was always in pristine condition. The hard court required less care, but was always clear of dirt and debris. Mac found that the ball machine was a great help in continuing her improvement. The cabin and the indoor courts were still under construction, so Mac practiced daily with the ball machine, making sure to practice her serve. She constantly worked on service disguise and with the advice of Scott and Anastasia's coach, was making excellent progress. Occasionally Mac would practice with a D-1 male player from the Pittsburg area. Many of these young men were probably more interested in dating Mac than they were in practicing tennis. Mac found a few to be interesting, but at 17, she knew she was too young to be dating 20-something young men. There would be time for that later.

When the cabin was occupant ready, Anastasia and her coach joined Mac for a week-long practice session on her hard court. Anastasia had improved since last year and would be a seeded player at Indian Wells. Mac, because she was ranked outside the top 100, would have to qualify. Anastasia's coach encouraged these training sessions with Mac, because he felt she had aided Anastasia's improvement. Of course these sessions also helped Mac, since she was able to absorb all the advice that was provided by an experienced international coach. After their one-week training block, Mac, Alice, Anastasia and her coach left Valley Head and arrived in Palm Springs on the same flight. They decided to stay in the same hotel to simplify practice schedules. When the draws were announced, Anastasia was seeded #18 and considered a contender for the singles title. Mac had to qualify, but she was ready and breezed through her two qualifying matches to make it into the main draw. Due to their US Open success, Mac and Anastasia were seeded #2 in the doubles.

Once Mac had gained the main draw, and playing on hard courts, she was in her comfort zone. She won the singles title and the doubles title with Anastasia. Mac collected 1.5 million dollars for her efforts. In singles, Anastasia lost in the quarters.

For Mac, Miami was a repeat of Indian Wells, Mac played brilliantly to again win the singles and the doubles titles. Mac collected another 1.5 million for her efforts. In singles, Anastasia lost in the semis. After a two-month long break, it was off to Roland Garros and the French Open.

L'Equipe, the French newspaper dedicated to sports, ran a full-page article on Mac's arrival in Paris. As the tournament progressed, every move by Alice and Mac was scrutinized by the French press. The French Open is commonly called Roland Garros, which is named for a French aviator, who died in combat in the final days of World War 1. The main stadium's roof is retractable and is named for French tennis player and journalist, Philippe Chatrier, who was instrumental in obtaining Grand Slam status for the event. The tournament is the only major that does not use Hawk-Eye Live to call lines, but instead depends on the chair umpire to inspect each disputed mark. Many in the tennis community have been critical of this controversial line calling and petitioned for Hawk-Eye Live. A 1,500-square-meter shopping center, located beneath courts 2 and 3, is a favorite for players and Mac was no exception. Expensive items would not dampen the enthusiasm of Mac and Alice when shopping at La Grande Boutique. There were three restaurants for players and their entourages. The main restaurant is located under court Philippe-Chatrier where players can find their favorite meals. The pasta bar was the favorite of Mac and Alice. New for the players is the recovery area, where protein shakes and tailored snacks are available for players after matches. There is also a quiet room which enables players to sleep, rest or meditate. Courts 15 and 16 are the only designated practice courts on the grounds. Accordingly, Mac and Anastasia arrived early to enjoy several practice sessions leading up to the start of the tournament.

Both Mac and Anastasia made it to the quarter-finals where they both lost close matches, but they did collect $430,000 apiece for their efforts. Mac lost to the #1 French player in front of a highly partisan crowd. The French had cheered for Mac earlier in the tournament, but in this match, they treated her like a villain. Mac played well in defeat, but was bothered by the unruly crowd. As always, Mac was gracious in defeat, and chalked up the loss as another learning experience. Mac and Anastasia won the doubles for their second Grand Slam title and collected $640,000. Their prize money total was the most that either player had ever won in a single tournament. During off days, Mac and Alice found time to visit the Eiffel Tower and the Notre Dame Cathedral. They both fell in love with Paris and vowed to return next year.

Now it was on to Wimbledon. With her quarter-final finish at the French Open, Mac's WTA ranking rose enough to qualify her for the main draw. This turned out to be an unfortunate turn of events since Mac had never played on grass and getting use to the bad bounces took some adjusting. Mac lost her first round match to a seeded player in three close sets, while Anastasia lost again in the quarter-finals. They dominated the doubles to win their third Grand Slam doubles title. By the time the tournament was over, Mac was comfortable on grass and $400,000 richer. The newspapers in Paris and London covered Mac's matches extensively and when Wimbledon concluded, Mac had gained celebrity status in Europe. Before returning to the US, Mac and Alice found time to do some shopping and sight-seeing.

At the US Open, Anastasia was seeded #15 and Mac #17. As a doubles pair they were seeded #1. The commotion around Mac had reached a fever pitch and Mac and Alice were forced to hire 24-hour security to keep paparazzi and souvenir seekers at bay. The media could not get enough of Mac and her mother. Fred decided to take some time off and fly to New York to join Alice and Mac. Fred thought this tournament might be special for Mac and he did not want to miss it. Of course he asked Mac and Alice if they would mind staying at his favorite hotel. Mac and Alice were happy to have Fred in New York and booked a suite at the Hilton. They both felt safer with Fred close by. It wasn't long until Fred sensed that their safety might be at risk. Something was not right with the security guy, Rodney. Fred noticed that Rodney would often stare at Mac during the rides to and from the Billie Jean Tennis Center. After checking with the NYPD, Fred found that Rodney not only had a lengthy criminal record but was a registered pedophile. With Mac and Alice safely in their suite, Fred confronted Rodney in the hallway and informed him that his services were no longer needed.

"Rodney, we will no longer need your services."
"Why? What's wrong?"
"Nothing's wrong. I'll just be taking over security now."
"But I need this job. I've been unemployed for months and I really need the money to feed my wife and kids."
"I'm sorry, but I know you're a registered pedophile with several felony convictions."
"You checked my background? You scum."
"I did and your services are no longer needed."
"You're going to regret this."
Expletives started to roll off Rodney's tongue and he yelled.
"You son of a bitch."

The yelling and cursing from both sides escalated until Rodney and Fred started throwing punches. Alice immediately called hotel security. The commotion in the hallway was so loud that people came out of their suites to see what was happening. As Rodney was led away by hotel security, he angrily screamed:

"I'll get you for this. I'll kill your ass and your women. You won't be safe anywhere; you piece of shit. You haven't heard the last of this. I have friends that kill for fun."
Once the ruckus was over, Fred coaxed the NYPD to provide them with a security detail, and everyone settled down for the evening meal. Despite having many invitations to play mixed doubles, Mac rightly decided that playing 3 events was too much and if she was going to win the singles and doubles with Anastasia, she would need all the mental and physical strength she possessed. During a practice session before the tournament was underway, Anastasia's coach Ivan, again

suggested to Mac and her parents that he would be honored to coach both players. This was the second time that Ivan had made this suggestion, but Mac always confirmed that Scott Flanagan was her coach and their collaboration would continue. He was just not available to travel. Once the tournament was underway, Mac easily won her first round singles match but Anastasia was upset by a qualifier from Germany. After the loss, Anastasia was an emotional wreck. Mac did her best to cheer her up, but to no avail. Anastasia and her coach had regarded this tournament to be her best opportunity to win a singles Slam and they were devastated.

After Mac and Anastasia won their first round doubles match, Mac continued to try and cheer up her partner. A dinner invitation was eventually accepted and room service for five was arranged in Mac's suite. Before long, Mac and Anastasia were laughing as if the loss had never happened and a good time was had by all.

The next day Mac faced an up-and-coming player from Argentina, who was a crafty baseliner who was able to mix up drop shots, slices and lobs, which pushed Mac to play her best tennis. Ashe Stadium was packed and they were witnessing a superb performance from both players. But the cunning baseliner was not the only foe that Mac faced that day. During a second set changeover, while Mac was seated on the player's bench, a half-naked climate protester stormed onto the court armed with a machete, and ran towards Mac. A glimpse of the protester out of the corner of her eye allowed Mac to barely avoid what could have been a fatal attack. The attacker took a swing at Mac and the reflexes and quickness of this world-class athlete were put to the test. Mac escaped the wild swing, but the machete found its mark in the meaty portion of Mac's upper thigh. After the attacker was wrestled to the ground by security, Mac's parents and medics rushed to her side. She required ten stiches and a heavy bandage to stop the bleeding and a doctor on site recommended that Mac retire. But once order was restored, Mac insisted that the match continue. Mac was shaken, but the horrified crowd had been jolted into a frenzy and roared their approval for every winner that came off Mac's racquet. Through sheer grit and the crowd's encouragement, Mac prevailed in three tough sets.

After the match, a visibly shaken Mac was consoled by Alice and Fred. Alice was ready to go home and take Mac with her. But Mac was intent on finishing what she started. There was no quit in Mac. After a night's stay for observation in a local hospital, doctors determined that the laceration did not cut into the muscle and Mac should expect a full recovery. Doctors did urge Mac to pull out of the tournament to avoid the chance of further injury. Her mother pleaded with Mac to quit. It was the first time Mac wanted to defy the wishes of her mother.

"Darling please, let's go home. It's not worth it. You have already proven yourself."
"I'm okay mom. You know I love you more than anything in the world, but this is something I must finish. I'll regret it forever if I quit now."
Fred's response was simple. "We're going home."
"I can't dad. I can't disappoint Anastasia and more importantly, I can't disappoint myself. The wound will heal."
In desperation, Alice shrieked: "You're going home."
A tearful Mac hugged her mom for a long time. Then she hugged her dad for a long time and then she hugged them both. With tears streaming done both cheeks, Mac sobbed: "I'm ready to go home."

Mac had finally realized that her desire to finish the tournament was selfish and her parents' wishes were right for obvious reasons. Fred notified tournament officials of Mac's decision and Mac called Anastasia. A perpetual gloom persisted over the remainder of the US Open. Under tight security, Mac and her parents were escorted to LaGuardia Airport and were promptly on their way home to WV. The protester was arrested by the NYPD and questioned. His lengthy criminal record revealed that he was a climate activist with severe mental problems. He was also a convicted felon who had served prison time for assault, but authorities could find no motivation for the attack on Mac.

On the plane ride back to WV, Mac and her parents were busy sorting through numerous offers of sponsorship deals for Mac. After a careful scrutiny of all offers, quality above quantity became the measuring stick for making final selections. Mac and her parents decided on five offers; Adidas apparel, Mercedes-Benz, Rolex, Nike and Wilson. All realized that fewer deals meant less money, but that had to be balanced against fewer time commitments for Mac. Mac would be turning 18 next year and eligible to play a full schedule on the WTA Tour. The media and the tennis community were disappointed to hear that there would be no Australian Open in Mac's immediate future. All agreed that in order to give Mac's leg time to completely heal, she should resume her quest for Wimbledon glory at next year's French Open. Mac was able to enjoy the holiday season with her family and friends and a New Year's celebration featured a fireworks display orchestrated by Fred. After ringing in the New Year, Mac felt ready to prepare for her trip to Paris.

Chapter 17

The two outdoor courts, the indoor court and cabin were now complete and Mac scheduled two training blocks with Anastasia and her coach. Anastasia seemed to be in good spirits, despite a first round loss at the Australian Open. Poor results in other events had adversely affected her singles ranking. She was however, still ranked in the WTA top hundred in singles and ranked #1 in doubles with Mac. She had tried playing with some other partners in doubles, but was unable to develop the synergy she had with Mac. Ivan, a former colonel in the Russian Army, had pushed Anastasia hard in the gym in an effort to make her stronger and faster. She was 29 years old and Ivan felt that time may be running out for her to make a big move in the rankings. Her movement was good but not great. Ivan had observed Mac's speed and quickness around the court and physically wanted the same for Anastasia. Ivan seemed to ignore the old maxim in tennis that says: 'You can make a slow player quicker but you can't make a slow player quick'. Because she had her own dreams of a singles Slam, Anastasia obeyed her coach and tried her best. Her desire to improve was as strong as ever. Mac was concerned that she might hurt herself and even cautioned Anastasia to cut back on some of her exercising. Ivan took umbrage with this unsolicited advice and his anger alarmed Mac.

But Mac was determined that this was going to be the year that she would achieve her dream. The quote above the entrance to Center Court at Wimbledon regularly danced in her head. "If you can meet with triumph and disaster and treat those two imposters just the same…" These two lines from Rudyard Kipling's inspirational poem 'If', seemed to speak directly to Mac. She had studied Kipling's literary work in one of her high school honors classes and was aware of the contrast between Kipling's horrific childhood and her own. She had already met with disaster in New York and now was ready to meet triumph at Wimbledon. Her training off the court consisted primarily of stretching, yoga and some agility running. She remembered Scott's advice that avoiding injury while seeking improvement was all important. Mac focused on improving her tennis skills by practicing specific shots with the aid of her ball machine. And she always practiced her serve.

Mac had five months before the start of the French Open and used her free time to fulfill commitments required in her endorsement contracts. Mac stayed busy with exhibitions, commercials, presentations and publicity campaigns. In return, Mac received some unexpected bonuses; a new Mercedes-Benz E-Class Convertible, multiple Adidas tennis outfits and the latest Rolex watch. These gifts were in addition to Mac's lucrative endorsement deals.

The months leading up to Roland Garros passed quickly and as Mac and Alice began packing for their trip to Paris. Alice seemed to be in a gloomy mood.

"What's wrong, Mom."
"I'm fine; just thinking."
"About what?"
"I was thinking about how badly the French fans treated you last year. They applauded every error you made."
"I was playing a French player. A lot of fans will root for their country's champion."
"I know, but it was still upsetting to watch. Your behavior on court was so wonderful and it didn't seem fair."
"I was perfectly okay with the crowd's enthusiasm for their player and as I told you afterwards, it was a good learning experience."

After a period of silence, Alice asked. "Should I take this outfit?
"It might feel good if it rains."

Anastasia got off to a disastrous start on the clay at Roland Garros, when she was forced to retire in the middle of her first round match due to injury. After running for a deep ball to the corner, she had severely pulled her hamstring. Because of the seriousness of the injury, she had to pull out of the doubles. Heartbroken, she wished Mac good luck before returning to Moscow. Ivan however, stayed behind and watched Mac's matches from her player's box. Mac thought it strange that Ivan didn't go back to Moscow with her. Mac texted and called Anastasia daily to check on her condition. The prognosis was not good. The MRI showed a grade 2 partial tear of her right hamstring that would not require surgery, but would take 4 to 8 weeks to heal. After a grueling rehabilitation, Anastasias' expected return to competitive tennis would likely take 3 to 6 months. Mac's empathy toward her Russian friend would help in her recovery. Mac promised to stay in touch and predicted another Slam doubles title in their future.

Mac's first round was an evening match on Court Suzanne-Lenglen, a court named after the French diva and icon of the 1930s. It was a rainy evening and the new retractable roof was closed. 10,000 spectators packed the stadium to view this teen upstart from WV. This was her first tournament appearance in 7 months and many were concerned she might be suffering from Post-traumatic stress disorder (PTSD), because of the machete attack at the US Open. As Mac entered the stadium, she waved to the crowd, blew kisses and flashed her dazzling smile. Her erect posture and athletic gait were those of a proud, confident young woman and erased all doubt of any effects of PTSD. The spectators gave Mac a long round of applause as she was introduced. After a brief warm-up with her qualifier opponent, Mac removed her warm-up to reveal a light-blue pleated skirt and a figure male fans would die for. Her mid-drift revealed a sculpted midsection putting her beauty on full display. Mac proceeded to deliver an exhibition of power and finesse that was rarely seen on the courts of Roland Garros. Mac demolished her hapless opponent 6-0 and 6-0 (known as a double bagel). The match lasted less than one hour, leaving many spectators wanting more. During the match, Mac's 10-inch machete scar was barely visible beneath the hemline of her skirt. Mac was simply stunning. Because of the machete attack on Mac in last year's US Open, all matches had security placed between the change-over benches and spectators. This was a welcome change and was duplicated by all Slams. Knowing that Mac would look fabulous in any apparel, Adidas supplied Mac with multiple outfits for every tournament. This was agreeable to Mac, since she liked to dress differently for each of her matches. Mac was always meticulous in her grooming and her attire, a trait taught her early on by her mother. Mac also packed numerous outfits for her days off and since she was no longer in the doubles, she and Alice would have more time to experience the sights and sounds of Paris. Security around Mac and Alice was tight and no one wanted a repeat of some random attack.

Since the next day was an off day, Mac and Alice headed for the practice courts for a morning workout. Mac was hoping someone might be available for a brief practice session. To her surprise, she had no trouble in finding suitable practice partners (mostly male) for the remainder of the tournament.

As Mac continued to progress through the draw, the fans were drawn to the electric elegance of this graceful cause célébre. Every match Mac played was sold out and the media had a field day with rumors of romantique involving Mac. When asked about her dating life in a post-match interview, she responded with a seductive smile. "There's a time for dating and a time to play tennis and now's the time to play tennis."

After 5 victories, Mac was in the semifinals playing on Court Philippe Chatrier in front of another sold-out night match. Her opponent was a crafty Brazilian and a protégé of the legendary Gustavo Kuerten. She was the #3 seed and possessed a variety of slices and drop shots. She was a worthy opponent and the best player Mac had played so far. After winning the first set 7-6, Mac was at a crucial stage in the second when the

Brazilian hit an angled drop shot which fooled Mac. Despite a late start, Mac sprinted forward and gracefully slid into the shot. Her front foot stuck in the damp clay and she pitched forward head first into the umpire's stand. The crowd gasped as Mac lay motionless face down on the red clay. Tournament officials, doctors and Alice sprinted to her side and were alarmed at what they saw. Blood was streaming down the side of Mac's face and dripping onto the clay. Mac was out cold. As the crowd watched in disbelief, medics carefully loaded Mac onto a stretcher and carted her out of the stadium to a waiting ambulance. On the way to the hospital and with Alice holding her hand, Mac momentarily regained consciousness and mumbled: "What happened mama?"

Fred had watched the incident on TV in horror and tried to call Alice immediately. Alice was slow to answer, but when she did, she was in panic mode.
"Fred, our baby's hurt. What should we do?"
"Pray right now, sweetheart."
"Fred, I can't think right now."
"Just calm down."
'I can't be calm. Fred, I can't be calm."
"Okay, do your best; keep me posted and I'll be there as soon as I can."

Mac spent two weeks in a Paris Hospital and was diagnosed with a severe concussion and a sprained neck. MRIs showed no fractures in either the skull or neck, but doctors were cautious in their prognosis. The neurologist told Alice and Fred that recovery from a severe concussion was hard to predict, but being a young strong athlete was to her advantage. He seemed to be more concerned about her neck sprain.

After spending a few days in a Paris hotel and under tight security, Mac and her parents returned home to Valley Head. The tennis world was in shock. Even though they realized that Mac's injury was a freak accident, there were calls to eliminate the umpires stand, or at least move it further from the net post. After a month of rest, Mac made a complete recovery. She had total mobility of her neck and resumed yoga and stretching in preparation for her next tournament. Her mother was not so sure. Mac assured her sponsors that she would resume playing in the French Open next year, but would skip the Australian.

"Honey, I can't take this anymore. No one would blame you if you quit playing."
"I would blame myself, mom. To win Wimbledon has been my dream for a long time."
"Are you sure this is want you want? What about marriage and a family?"
"I'm quite sure. I'm only 19. Marriage and family can wait."

Chapter 18

They met in church and this chance encounter with a stranger would alter the course of Mac's life. He accidently bumped into Mac after the morning church service. Mac was not sure if it was an accident, but she accepted the stranger's apology.

"I am so sorry. How clumsy of me. Is there anything I can do to make it up to you? My name is Evan and you are?"

Mac looked Evan up and down and coolly responded. "My name is Mackenzie." She judged Evan to be about 6' 2", medium build and not particularly attractive. He had brown eyes and curly brown hair and Mac was surprised that Evan didn't know her name. Most people she encountered were well-aware of her tennis accomplishments and her celebrity status. She had never seen this young man before and guessed he was a visitor. Evan, on the other hand was smitten by Mac's obvious beauty and was having a hard time expressing himself. As Evan continued to mumble aimlessly, Mac did hear one thing loud and clear.

"Would you like to go out to dinner with me?"
"I don't know you."
"I'm a graduate of Penn State and new to the area. I'm 22 years old and never been married. I would be honored to tell you more over dinner."

Mac was rarely speechless, but at this moment, she was. He seemed harmless, shy, but well-mannered and well-groomed. Mac didn't think him a serial killer, so on a whim, she said:

"Okay, but only for lunch."
"Do you know a good place?"
"Most of the restaurants in Snowshoe are closed this time of year. I do know the Route 66 Restaurant and Board Shop is open for lunch on Saturday. It's about 10 miles from our house."
"That is fine with me. I'll pick you up at 11:30."
"Okay."

At 11:30 sharp, Evan arrived at Mac's doorstep. After introducing him to her parents. Mac declared:

"Mom, Evan and I are going out for lunch and we should be back by 2 pm at the latest."

Evan had parked his 10-year old Toyota next to Mac's convertible. He had not seen a Mercedes convertible in this part of WV and wondered who might own this type of car. Mac noticed him giving the convertible the once-over and asked if he would like to take the Mercedes. After an enthusiastic yes, he proceeded to hold the driver-side door open for Mac. She calmly said:

"You can drive."
"Are you sure? It looks like an expensive car. Is it your parent's car?"
"No, it's mine."

On the way to the restaurant, Evan wondered how Mac could afford this expensive car and Mac wanted to know more about Evan. Consequently not much was said and each tried to figure the best way to break the ice. Finally, Evan inquired:

"I'm not sure how to ask this and not come across as being overly forward."
"Go ahead."
"How can you afford an expensive car like this?"
"I've been blessed."
"You didn't steal it? Did you?"
"No."
"A loan?"
"No."
"Um… A wealthy relative?"
"If I tell you, can we talk about something else?"
"Okay."
"It was a gift."

An awkward silence lingered for the rest of the drive. Once at the diner, Mac was aware of Evan staring at her and it made her uncomfortable. Mac was the first to break the silence.

"Why are you staring at me?"

"I'm sorry. You're just so gorgeous, it's hard not to stare."

"Thank you, but staring makes me uncomfortable. Tell me something about yourself? Are you employed in the area?"

"Yes, I work as a computer analyst for a large construction company."

"And what does a computer analyst do?"

"We make sure that all computer systems within our organization work efficiently to achieve our company goals."

"Wow that's impressive. You must have a degree or two in order to do that job."

"I graduated high school at 16 and enrolled at Penn State in an accelerated engineering program. I graduated with multiple degrees in economics, engineering and physics. I'm sorry. I didn't mean to brag. It's just that people…"

"Now you're trying to impress me. How long have you been working with this company?"

"On Monday, it will be 4 weeks. But enough about me. What about you?"

"There's not much to tell. I am an only child and I've lived with my parents in Valley Head my entire life. Attending church is a big part of my life and I enjoy playing tennis. Now tell me more about you?"

"I am also an only child and I enjoy church activities, but I've never played tennis. In fact, I'm not much of an athlete or sport's fan."

"You're tall. You might make a good tennis player."

Evan couldn't help himself for occasionally staring at Mac. Her bright blue eyes and engaging smile would set any young man's heart to pounding and he was no exception. Mac was struck by Evan's education and impressed with his manner. She couldn't help but like him a little bit, but only as a friend. Evan, on the other hand, wanted to be more than just a friend and was already planning a second date. She just seemed too good to be true. On the way back to Valley Head, they engaged in some light chatter, but not much else. As Evan followed her up the steps leading to the front door, he couldn't help but notice the graceful curve of her back beneath the smoothness of her silky dress.

"MacKenzie, would you go on a second date with me? This time for dinner at the Appalachian Kitchen in Snowshoe?"
"I'm flattered, but I don't think so. I don't really date and I have to start training for my next tournament."
"As in tennis?"
"Yes, I haven't played for a while and am anxious to resume training."
"Well, if not dinner, what about showing me a thing or two about tennis?"
"I don't know…"
"I'll promise to be the best student you've ever had."
"Ah… Well, I'll meet you here tomorrow at 9 am. Bring your sneakers."
"Okay. See you then."

Evan could barely wait to grab his phone and Google MacKenzie/tennis. He was astonished at what he found. Pictures of this fascinating beauty were all over the internet. She was famous and rich; very rich. Evan suddenly realized that the threshold for being a serious boyfriend would be high and it would take a herculean effort on his part to make it happen. The next day Evan bounded up the four wooden steps, stepped onto the wrap-around porch and quietly knocked on the front door. He was ready to play some tennis. Mac answered the door carrying a large Wilson tennis bag. She was dressed in an Adidas outfit that accentuated every curve of her figure. She was quite a sight and suddenly Evan was nervous. He hadn't been nervous before, but that was before he knew she was a celebrity. Mac sensed his nervousness and gently said:

"What's wrong? You look like you've seen a ghost."
"I think maybe I have."
"No you haven't. Follow me and we'll go around back and hit some tennis balls."

Following Mac was a treat and Evan's eyes did not miss a curve. As they rounded the corner of the house, two manicured tennis courts graced the back yard. Mac motioned him over to the reddish court and unzipped her bag.

"Let's play on this one. You can borrow one of my racquets."
"MacKenzie, before we start, I have to confess that I searched you on the Internet and found that you are not just a tennis player, but a world champion and I am thoroughly intimidated."
"There's no need to be, Evan. I'm a human being just like you."
"That makes me feel slightly better, but I want you to know that my interest in you has nothing to do with your fame or money. I find you fascinating and I enjoy your company."
"Okay... Now I'm going to turn on the ball machine. Stand behind me and watch me hit a few balls. Then you can copy. Are you right-handed."
"Yes."

After pulling two racquets from her bag and giving one to Evan, she proceeded to demonstrate the forehand and backhand. Mac had a remote for the ball machine and set it so it alternated from side to side. Evan stood behind Mac and watched in admiration. After turning off the ball machine, Mac said:

"Okay. It's your turn."

"It looks like fun, but I'll probably embarrass myself."

"You'll do fine."

Mac turned on the ball machine and after a few misses, Evan started hitting the ball on the strings and over the net. The longer Evan hit, the better he got. Mac thought to herself. He's a better athlete than I thought. With a little practice, he could be pretty good. After a few minutes, Evan had broken a sweat and decided to take a rest on the courtside bench.

"Why don't I watch you hit, while I catch my breath."

"Okay, I'll hit a few more and then we can practice the serve."

While seated on the bench and after a two-hour practice session, Mac offered Evan a towel. With her own towel, she preceded to dry her silky arms and legs. Evan noticed and found it hard to keep from gawking, but thought this might be a good time to ask for a second date.

"MacKenzie, would you like to have dinner with me at the Appalachian Kitchen on Saturday night. I hear it's one of the finest restaurants in Snowshoe."

"No, I don't think so. You're nice to ask, but I really don't have time to date."

"You don't have to think of it as a date; just dinner."

"No, I can't. Besides, it's very expensive."

"Mac, I have a good job that pays well and I can afford to pay. It will be my treat for showing me how to play tennis."

"I really don't have time for a boyfriend or dating."

"Is there anything I can say to change your mind?"

"I don't think so, but I do know that I'm thirsty. How about a glass of iced tea. We can sit on the porch and critique your tennis game."

"Good Idea. Can I help with the tea?"

"No, just have a seat in a rocker and I'll get us a couple of glasses."

While his body was relaxing, Evan's mind was racing. His overtures toward Mac weren't working. What could he say to interest her in a second date? Several minutes later, Mac brought out two glasses of iced tea, complete with a lemon slice and sat down in the rocker beside Evan. They both were sipping their iced teas, when he asked:

"You've achieved so much in tennis. Do you have any goals left that you want to accomplish?"

"Yes. My dream is to win Wimbledon."

"That's the grass court tournament in England. Right?"

"Yes and it's a tricky surface to play on, but I believe I have improved enough to be a real threat on grass. What about you? Do you have any dreams?"

"Yes. I would like to start my own software company and develop software capable of regulating the temperatures of nuclear fusion reactors."

"Hasn't that already been done?"

"No. Not for fusion reactors. Fission, yes, but the future is fusion power plants, which have the potential to produce an unlimited amount of cheap electricity with little or no waste. In time, I believe there will be a global push to have fusion plants in all parts of the world and that could go a long way in reducing global warming."

"That's an impressive dream. Is it achievable?"

"I think it is. It may take 10-20 years, but I believe it will happen."

Mac grew silent and pondered what Evan had said. Up until now, she had never felt an attraction to Evan and she still didn't. But she might want to get to know him better. He broke the silence by saying:

"Is there a chance that you might reconsider my offer of dinner?"

"Okay. I will reconsider on one condition."

"What condition is that?"

"That it won't be a date. It will just be dinner with a friend."

"I'm already your friend, but I would like it to be more."

"I've told you before. I don't have time for a boyfriend."

"Okay, let's try it your way. I'll pick you up Saturday at 7 p.m. May I call you Mac?"

"Sure. See you Saturday."

On Saturday morning, it was snowing heavily and by 7 p.m, it was below freezing and the roads were treacherous. In case of bad weather, Evan had snow tires on his Toyota and felt somewhat prepared. Once arriving at Mac's doorstep, the roads had turned icy and Evan had an uneasy feeling about the road conditions. Mac answered the door and offered this suggestion:

"My dad said that we can take his new Ford-150 truck. He has chains on the tires, four-wheel drive and felt it would be the safest option on the icy mountain roads. Will that be okay with you?"

"That would be more than okay. I was feeling a bit uneasy about my Toyota making it up the mountain."

"Good, and you can drive."

On the way to Appalachia Kitchen, the conversation was light and filled with laughter. In addition to being a good listener, Evan had a way with words and Mac was starting to enjoy his company. Their reservation was at 7:30, so Mac opted to call ahead and let the hostess know they would be late. Mac and Evan were fortunate to have a short walk to the restaurant's entrance, since the wind brought the wind chill down into the high teens. Once seated, they realized they were practically alone. The weather had caused numerous cancellations, and combined with soft piano music, the atmosphere was perfect for a relaxed conversation. When Mac removed her hoodie to reveal her long silky auburn hair, Evan couldn't help but stare. He had only seen her in a ponytail and this was a surprise.

"You're staring again."

"I know and I'm sorry. I just can't seem to help myself,"

"I might stare at you for a while and see if it makes you uncomfortable."

"You can try, but your bright blue eyes may betray you."

"How so?"

"You must know what Shakespeare had to say about the eyes."

"What did he say?"

"Shakespeare put it this way. "Eyes are the windows to the soul." Psychologists say that it reveals the emotions and intentions of the owner."

"Maybe I shouldn't stare. What about your dating life?"

"I seldom go on dates and have never had a girlfriend. I took a vow of chastity when I was quite young and made the decision to save myself for marriage. At times, I've been tempted but I made that decision for religious reasons and I would like to marry someone with the same belief."

"I knew I shouldn't stare."

"Why, Mac? Are you afraid you might reveal a secret?"

"I guess I might."

"Sometime, I would like to know your secret, but you don't have to tell me now."

The dinner progressed without any more major reveals, but they certainly enjoyed each other's company. The conversation was filled with laughter and the food was good too. On the way home, the roads had worsened and it was slow going down the mountain road. Mac texted ahead to let her parents know she would be home past her 11 p.m. curfew. They arrived just after midnight. It was still snowing, but the wind had died down some. As they stood on the porch, Evan was hoping for that signal that a relationship might be in his future. Mac gave him a quick peck on the cheek and disappeared into the house. On the short drive back to Mingo, Evan wondered what was next. He knew the date had gone well, but then he remembered. He forgot to ask for another date.

Chapter 19

The following day, Evan phoned Mac and inquired about a second date on Saturday.

"Would you be available for dinner this Saturday?"
"No I can't, I will be in Charleston for a 3-week training session and won't be available. But you can call me back in three weeks."
"May I text you while you're in Charleston?"
"Sure, but make it in the evening. I should be finished with training by then."
"Okay and good luck with your training."

The three weeks went by slowly for Evan, but he texted Mac every night and stayed busy with his work duties. Mac was able to sharpen all areas of her game at Scott Flanagan's new

Academy. Scott had saved a two-bedroom apartment for Mac and had a slew of top players at the Academy for Mac to train with. Scott also gave Mac some pointers on disguising her serve. During their daily texting and some encouragement from Evan, Mac agreed to a movie date when she returned to Valley Head.

Upon her return, Mac and Evan enjoyed a romantic comedy at the Cinemark Theater in Elkins. After an evening snack, they returned to Valley Head and Mac's porch. This time Evan didn't wait for a signal from Mac. After looking into her bright blue eyes, he pulled her close and gave her a long wet kiss on the lips. Mac seemed confused, but Evan could tell she liked it. This time he didn't forget.

"Mac, are you available next Saturday?"
"I might be. Who's asking?"
"I am, silly."
"Okay, but I can only go out on Saturday nights. Roland Garros starts in four weeks and I will be busy."

Mac and Evan grew increasingly closer over the next four weeks and their physical contact became more frequent and more passionate. Finally Mac confessed her hidden feelings.

"Evan, I like you a lot, but I have a conundrum to confess. I also took a vow of chastity for religious and moral reasons. I want to stay a virgin until I marry the person I love."
"Mac, you are my dream match. I have prayed that our outlook on the subject would be the same. I want you to know that your confession in no way lessens my physical attraction towards you and I will not betray your trust. I was concerned

that there were no attractive women left that shared my beliefs. Can I consider you my one and only girlfriend?"

"Yes you may."

"You have made me the luckiest guy in the world. I promise to stay in touch while you are in Paris and London and will look forward to watching you on TV."

For two young people to have the same views on religion and chastity were rare in this modern era, but Mac and Evan were exceptional individuals and to find each other was special.

A week later Mac and Alice were off to Paris. Mac had a small private jet housed in Elkins and a pilot on call. The jet was large enough for one king-sized bed, a kitchen and shower facilities. It was convenient for Mac and her mom, because they didn't have to worry about security until she arrived in Paris. Once they landed at Charles de Gaulle (CDG) Airport, they met their security team and were whisked away to the Le Belgrand Hotel. With great views of the Eiffel Tower, the Hilton property was a five-minute ride to Roland Garros.

With the retirement of Anastasia, Mac entered the singles only. Her first round opponent was a rising young star from Mexico and rumored to be the girlfriend of a powerful drug lord. Her name was Maria and she was touted as Mexico's best chance for a major championship. Ironically, Mac received several death threats before her opening match. Receiving anonymous threats or marriage proposals were nothing new to Mac, so she was not overly concerned. Her mother, however, was worried.

After a year's absence, Mac walked onto Court Philippe Chatrier to a thunderous applause from a sold-out crowd. She was given a standing ovation that lasted nearly two minutes. Unknown to Mac, the drug lord and a couple of his cronies were in Maria's player box. The box was so loud and unruly that security had to be called. Two *amigos* were escorted out of the arena for yelling obscenities at Mac. When the match started, many in the stadium wondered if the injuries suffered a year earlier would have a negative effect on Mac's performance. It didn't take long for that question to be answered. Mac was on fire and obliterated her hapless opponent in 58 minutes. In the packed press room after the match, reporters jockeyed for the attention of this charismatic beauty from WV. The first question was from a New York Times reporter:

"Mac, you played beautifully today. After being away from tournament competition for so long, were you nervous at the start of the match?"
"Excited maybe, but not nervous."
"Your game is so powerful and graceful at the same time. To what do you contribute your excellence on the clay?"
"Whatever talent I have is a gift from God."
"…You were so dominant today. Were you trying to send a message to an obviously talented young player?"
"Not at all. I was just trying to do my best."
"Everyone wants to know if you are dating someone?"
"Yes, I have a boyfriend."
"Can you tell us who the lucky fellow is?"
"No, I can't. My personal life is private."

As Evan witnessed the press interview from afar, he couldn't help but beam with pride. While he knew he was blessed, he was elated for Mac. He called Mac every evening and especially loved listening to Mac talk about the sights and sounds of Paris. She enjoyed hearing about Evan's job and would sometimes recount the day's match. Every call ended with: I love you.

The fact that Mac had a boyfriend was big news in Paris, especially in the tabloids. The gossip was outrageous and Mac was rumored to be involved with everyone from Hollywood's most eligible bachelors to European royalty.

Sometime later in Mexico City, Maria's reported boyfriend was being interviewed by Excelsior TV. The suspected leader of Mexico's largest drug cartel was agitated and angrily shouted that Mac had tried to embarrass his Maria. He also complained that the partisan French crowd had unfairly affected the outcome. Before leaving the studio, he looked squarely into the camera and warned Mac with a string of profanities that she would pay for this humiliation.

Mac easily won her next five matches in straight sets and in the final was paired with her former antagonist, Emma. Mac retained a vivid memory of her last encounter with Emma and the brawl that ensued. Emma's dad was serving a one year suspension by the International Tennis Federation (ITF) and was not in attendance. Emma had been the top American player for the last two years, but had never won a major. The French Open Final would be contested between two Americans and Mac was eager to play her best.

On the morning of the Final, Mac was under the weather. She had finally succumbed to the damp rainy weather that had played havoc with the scheduling. She had developed a bad cold and cancelled her mid-morning practice session. Instead, she opted to rest in her suite until noon. Mac arrived at the tournament site in time to stretch and take in some extra hydration. Upon entering the stadium, Mac received her usual thunderous ovation. Court Philippe Chatrier was packed and the crowd was anxious to see a well-played match between these two young Americans. Mac got off to a slow start and lost the first set 6-2. Emma sensed that Mac was a bit sluggish and proceeded to run her relentlessly from side to side. With the crowd behind her, Mac hung on to win the second set tiebreaker and then started to find her groove. To the delight of the crowd, she closed out the match by the score of 2-6, 7-6 and 6-3. At the conclusion of the match, there was no hugging at the net and the hand shake was no more than a blur. Mac then climbed up into the player's box and hugged both her parents. Fred had flown in for the Finals and had arrived just in time to witness Mac's first Slam Singles Title. Emma was livid, but Mac was the French Open Champion.

At the awards ceremony, Mac held the pure silver Coupe Suzanne-Lenglen trophy high over her head as she beamed a mega-watt smile to the French crowd. She then gave her acceptance speech in both French and English. She thanked the crowd, her parents and gave high praise for the effort and talent of Emma. She maintained that Emma would have many more opportunities for Slam titles. As Mac heaped praise on Emma, Emma's countenance softened and her anger was replaced with a slight admiration of Mac.

After Mac's French Open victory, Mac fulfilled several commitments, including a photo shoot with Rolex and a clinic for underprivileged youngsters. The clinic was co-sponsored by Wilson and Adidas. Between commitments, Mac and her parents stayed mostly in their suite and celebrated with some excellent French food. Quiche Lorraine, Galettes and Crêpes were their favorites. Since there was three weeks before the start of Wimbledon, Mac and her parents decided to return to WV for a much-needed rest. They were met at the Elkins Airport by Evan, who was still pumped up over Mac's French Open victory. Hugs were enjoyed by everyone and the trip back to Valley Head in Mac's newest Mercedes was filled with merriment.

During the next two weeks, Mac and Evan grew closer and Mac's practice sessions were less frequent. Mac enjoyed the time off and the reprieve from the constant spotlight. The time away from fans, paparazzi and security was a welcome change and resulted in a happy period for Mac. She felt good physically and mentally and had a boyfriend who shared her values. She was playing well and ready to achieve her dream. What could possibly go wrong?

Four days before the start of Wimbledon, Mac and Alice flew from Elkins on Mac's private jet and landed at the London Gatwick Airport. Upon arrival, they met their security team and took the short walk to the Hilton London Gatwick Hotel. After checking into their suite, Mac made arrangements for some practice sessions at The Boodles. Founded in 2002, The Boodles is a five-day tennis event held on the regal grounds of Stoke Park in Buckinghamshire. The event enables the British rich and famous to mix and mingle with the world's top tennis players. The New York Times described the event as 'unlike nearly anything else on the tennis calendar...a Gatsby-like few days on an estate outside London. The event is named for the English luxury jeweler Boodles and is the perfect English garden party. The stadium is designed so that every seat is within 10 meters of the court. Mac decided not to enter the exhibition tournament, but would loosen up on the grass practice courts instead.

When Mac and Alice arrived at The Boodles for her practice session, the practice courts were taken, so she and Alice took a courtside seat and watched a few of the European players go through their practice routine. It didn't take long for a top male player to ask Mac if she wanted to "hit a few". Soon after, the courtside seats were full and there was standing room only to watch this graceful American glide around the court smacking tennis balls as only she could. After her hitting session, wealthy and connected Brits crowded around Mac to get a closer view of this elegant American sensation. Up close and in person, Mac was a radiant jewel with all the charm, wit and charisma expected of a megastar. Alice attempted to stay out of the limelight, but was unable to avoid a host of male admirers eager to make her acquaintance.

With the exception of Mac's daily practice sessions at The Boodles, Mac and Alice stayed mostly in their suite, ordered room service and sampled the English cuisine. Their favorites were shepherd's pie, beef Wellington and the Victoria sandwich. Alice liked the London Fog (Earl Grey Tea latte) and Mac loved the Wimbledon staple: strawberries and cream.

Since Wimbledon requires players to wear all white, designers at Adidas had designed two stunning white dresses tailored just for Mac. And as usual, Mac did the people at Adidas proud. She was not only gorgeous, but the outfit was a perfect match for her magnetic personality. Due to her protected ranking and her victory at Roland Garros, Mac was Wimbledon's #10 seed. Her opening round opponent was an English veteran, who had been a former Wimbledon semi-finalist. Despite the partisan crowd and the challenges of the grass surface, Mac prevailed in three tough sets. In her on-court interview, Mac thanked everyone, praised her opponent and hoped that her first singles victory on grass would not be her last. Playing only singles, Mac methodically progressed through the draw. As she became comfortable on the tricky grass surface, she began playing with more conviction and won her semi-final match in straight sets in less than 90 minutes. With the absence of English players, the crowd was now solidly behind Mac and she did not disappoint. During her semi-final match, Mac noticed that Emma's father was seated directly behind her opponent's player box. His suspension had ended and his combative nature was on full display as he watched Mac dominate her opponent. Mac was on a roll and in the finals was heavily favored against her American rival Emma.

Back in WV, Evan and Fred were enjoying the matches on Fred's big-screen TV. Fred and Evan both knew their way around the kitchen and had their own version of *Breakfast at Wimbledon*. Because of the five hour time difference between London and WV, most of Mac's matches were in the morning in Valley Head. Their favorite breakfast became buckwheat pancakes topped with maple syrup and a side of sausage. Every Mac victory was celebrated with the Wimbledon staple: strawberries and cream. Fred and Evan were becoming close buddies and shared a mutual respect for each other's talent and work ethic.

Meanwhile back in London, Mac decided to forego practice on her off day before the finals. Instead, she and Alice decided to visit a nearby spa for a massage and manicure. Returning to the hotel under tight security, they ordered room service. Mac ordered shepherd's pie and strawberries and cream and Alice ordered the Victoria sandwich with an Earl Grey Tea latte. It was 8 p.m. and room service was running late. Mac called the front desk to inquire why room service was so slow. She was told there was a staffing problem, but their food would be there shortly. At 8:30, there was a knock on the door:

"This is security. Your room service is here."
Alice opened the door and a white-clad steward rolled in a room service trolley and unexpectedly shut the door. Mac suddenly sensed that something was wrong. Mac did not recognize the steward and inquired:

"Do you have the right room?"
"Si, right room."

Suddenly the intruder calmly pulled out a hand gun and said:

"I not kill you. I only shoot in knee."
"No, no, nooo." Alice screamed.

As the intruder aimed his gun toward Mac, Alice stepped between them and was shot point-blank in the abdomen. Alice collapsed into Mac's arms and with blood everywhere, the gunman rushed past security and fled down the hallway. As Mac held a badly wounded Alice, security belatedly rushed into the room to see what the commotion was about.

Mac shrieked to security: "Call 911"

It was 1:30 p.m. in Valley Head when Mac called Fred:
A sobbing Mac screamed: "Mom's been shot."
"What?"
"Mom's been shot and medics are on the way."

155

"How bad is it?"
"Real bad."
"Is she alive?"
"I think so."
"Try to stay calm and I'll be there as soon as I can."
"I can't stay calm, dad! Mom's been shot and may be dead. What can I do?"
"I'm on my way."

When the news of the shooting became known, the situation became crazy. Police, media and curious onlookers were everywhere. Mac rode in the ambulance with Alice, while the medic administered CPR. Once in the hospital, Alice was taken to ER and immediately underwent an exploratory laparotomy (a surgical procedure that gains access to the abdominal cavity). Doctors informed Mac that Alice had died on the operating table from severe bleeding of the aorta. After penetrating the aorta, the bullet had lodged in the spine.

Meanwhile, back in WV, Fred and Evan drove to Charleston and chartered a flight to London. 15 hours later, they were with Mac in a different hotel. Once Mac saw Fred and Evan, she began crying incessantly and despite their best efforts, Mac could not be comforted. Mac had lost her mama and Fred had lost his first and only love. Fred and Alice had been married for 35 years and Fred was heartbroken. Through a flood of tears, Mac blurted out:

"Dad, this can't be happening."
"Sweetheart, we have to get through this."
"Mom's last words to me were; I love you sweetheart and take care of Fred"

Upon hearing Alice's last instruction, Fred burst into tears. Soon afterwards, all three were hugging and crying together. The hotel suite was filled with despair and very little was said during a mostly sleepless night. The next morning, Fred wanted to visit the hospital and say his goodbyes to Alice. Mac and Evan opted to stay in the hotel to make arrangements for the flight back home. Mac was questioned several times by Scotland Yard and they assured Mac they would find the individual responsible. Amid tight security, the grieving threesome was off to WV on Mac's private jet.

Chapter 20

$\mathcal{O}$nce back home in Valley Head and for the next several months, Fred and Alice remained at the house and only allowed Evan to visit. Evan performed all the shopping and did his best to comfort Mac. Mac mostly refused to eat and fell into a deep depression. Fred fared just slightly better. They both questioned their faith, quit going to church and wondered how God could let this happen. Mac lost weight and after 6 months was a frail-looking portrait of her former self. She cut her long silky hair, stayed mostly in her pajamas and with the exception of Scotland Yard and a few of her sponsors, cut off all contact with the outside world. In spite of all that had happened, her sponsors remained committed and reasoned that Mac would eventually be able to continue her commitments and her tennis. Evan was frustrated with his inability to console Mac. After doing a great deal of research, Evan decided to purchase a yellow Labrador Retriever puppy in the hopes of brightening Mac's spirit. He selected North Fork Labrador Retriever located in St Albans, WV for his purchase. His selection was based on their reputation and the fact that their puppies were registered with the American Kennel Club (AKC). Additionally all North Folk puppies were certified by the Orthopedic Foundation for Animals (OFA), the Certified Eye Registry Foundation (CERF) and OptiGen progressive retinal atrophy (PRA) tested. Evan also figured that if for some reason, Mac didn't want the puppy, he could nurture the pup himself. When the big day arrived, Evan told Mac he had a surprise for her. He carried the yellow Lab puppy in a small dog crate with a yellow bow on top and announced to Mac:

"I hope you like her."
Momentarily Mac was speechless. "…She's beautiful. Can I keep her?"
"You bet you can. She's yours."
"Does she have a name?"
"No. You can name her."
"I think I will call her Precious."

Mac gave Evan a quick peck on the cheek. It wasn't much, but was the first sign of affection that Mac had shown towards Evan in six months. As Mac held the 6-week old puppy in her arms, she said:
"I will take good care of you."

The next day, Evan asked Mac if she would like to go to Elkins and shop for some puppy supplies. Mac would need a doggie bed, feeding bowls and puppy food. Evan knew Mac had not left the house in 6 months and was hoping a trip to Elkins would help break the spiral of depression that had taken over Mac's life.

"Would you like to drive to Elkins with me to get some needed items for Precious?"

"I don't know. I haven't been out for a while."

"Are you sure? A change of scenery might do you good."

"Well, okay. Give me a few minutes to get dressed." A short while later, Mac immerged from her bedroom and exclaimed: "Okay, I'm ready."

"I think you'll need your coat. It's 20 degrees outside."

Minutes later, Mac appeared in a warm winter coat. "Okay, now I'm ready and you can drive the Mercedes."

On the drive to Elkins, Evan was happy to have some alone time with Mac and made the most of it. Trying his best to be upbeat, he talked primarily about her puppy, but Mac remained mostly distant. Once they were in Elkins and had finished shopping for Precious, Mac decided she needed a haircut. This excited Evan, since this was the first indication that Mac was starting to take an interest in her appearance. Once in the salon, Mac requested a blunt bob hairstyle. It wasn't exactly Evan's favorite, but it was a start. On the way back to Valley Head, Evan complimented her haircut, but she was still detached. Mac was anxious to get back to Precious.

As the days turned to weeks, Mac's depression lifted slightly and Evan was able to spend more time with her. She began to eat more regularly and Evan, Mac and Fred started attending church services on Sunday. Mac refused to go out to dinner or on dates. Instead, she preferred evenings on the porch or scenic drives in her convertible. Physical contact was minimal and any emotional connection competed with Precious, who was Mac's constant companion. Mac claimed that Evan was still her boyfriend and she loved him, but Evan knew it was not the same as before. Evan was sure that Mac suffered from post-traumatic stress disorder (PTSD). She had all the indicators. Flashbacks, nightmares and severe anxiety plagued Mac on a regular basis. The difficulty of maintaining a close relationship with Mac was demanding, but Evan was determined to return their connection to some sense of normalcy.

A chance encounter while grocery shopping threatened to change the trajectory of Evan's life. It started innocently enough, when a young woman asked for help in reaching a box of cereal. Evan was nearby and was happy to help. It was only after retrieving the box that he noticed the appearance of this young lady. She was well-groomed, well-dressed and possessed a figure to match. In short, she was an alluring female. Upon leaving the store, he saw the same pretty maid staring at a flat tire. Evan asked if he could help and ended up changing the flat. It was a cold winter day and Evan only had a light jacket, but it was an easy fix and so as Evan prepared to leave, the woman said:

"Please let me pay you."
"No, it was not a problem. Glad to help."
"But I insist. At least let me buy you a cup of coffee. It will help you warm up."
"Well, okay if there's a place nearby, but I'm on a tight schedule."
"I know just the place."

Over a cup of coffee, Evan learned that this brown-eye maiden with long brown hair was a 22-year-old widow, whose husband had been killed in a mining accident two years earlier. Her name was Olivia and Evan rightly guessed her to be Hispanic. There was something about her that Evan found appealing. So when Olivia asked an out of the way question, Evan was startled.

"Would you like to go out for dinner sometime?"

"No, I really can't. I have a girlfriend."

"I know who you are and that you date MacKenzie. I also can see why you are one of the most eligible bachelors in Randolph County."

"You flatter me, but I have dated Mac for a long time and I am trying to help her recover from the horrible death of her mother."

"I read about her mother in the news. MacKenzie must be devastated."

"She is and her progress has been slow."

"It might help if you had someone to talk to. It wouldn't have to be a date. We could just go as friends."

"Just as friends?"

"Sure, and we could talk about anything you want."

"Well..., okay, I guess it wouldn't hurt if we went out as friends. I'll pick you up Monday at 7."

It was soon Monday and Evan wondered if he was doing the right thing. He would need to tell Mac and hoped that she would understand. After all, it was just dinner with a friend, albeit an enticing one. Olivia had no children and lived by herself in a small house near Mingo. Evan was there promptly at 7 and was surprised when Olivia answered the door. She was more seductive than he remembered.

"Wow, you look..."

What's the matter?"

"Nothing. Nothing at all. You look incredible."

"I hope you mean that in a good way."
"Oh, yes, in a very good way."
"Well, thank you. You look nice too."

On the way to Elkins, Olivia was an animated talker and Evan seemed to enjoy her company. Her sparkling personality showed through in every movement and expression. She confided to Evan that her ex-husband was an older man with considerable wealth and included in his marriage proposal were promises of a secure future. The 18-year-old orphaned Olivia cautiously accepted. Their short marriage had been okay, but lacked the spark one might expect from two newly-weds. Once seated in the restaurant, Evan had a chance to study her delicate oval face. She had full luscious lips and her big brown eyes seemed to twinkle as she spoke. Evan was smitten and he couldn't help himself.

"I find you dangerously irresistible."
"What do you mean?"
"I'm not sure what I mean. I just know that you are a seductive beauty and that could spell trouble."
"I think I'm flattered. How could that spell trouble?"
"I'm lucky to have you as just a friend."

The drive back to Mingo was uneventful, but Evan's mind was conflicted. He was physically attracted to Olivia, but his vow of chastity loomed large. When Evan walked Olivia to her door, she promptly invited him inside to warm up.

"Why don't you come inside and I will make us some coffee?"
"Okay, but I can't stay long. I have a big job to bid tomorrow and I have to get up early."

"If you throw a few logs on the fire, I will make us a couple of cups of coffee."

Evan made himself at home and observed his surroundings. Her home was neatly furnished, clean and comfortable. The warmth emanating from the fireplace prompted him to remove his coat. When Olivia returned with coffee, Evan had no trouble noticing the ample curves that filled out her dress. As they sipped their coffee, Evan began talking about his feelings for Mac and confessed that he had taken a vow of chastity that was important to him and to Mac. Olivia patiently listened, but she had other thoughts on her mind. She suddenly excused herself and told Evan:

"Don't move. I'll be right back."
"Okay, but I need to leave soon."

When Olivia returned she had on a see-through nightie that left nothing to the imagination. She sat down on the sofa beside Evan and amid the smell of her soft perfume, looked squarely into his confused eyes.

"Do you like what you see?"
"I do, but we're just friends; right?"
"I hope we are, but friends can enjoy each other, can't we."

Impulsively, Olivia kissed him square on the lips. Not once, but twice and then again. Evan responded and soon they were in Olivia's bed. Sometime later, Evan was no longer a virgin. The next morning Evan woke with a start. He was late for work. Evan's world had been turned upside down. He knew he had broken Mac's trust. He had broken his vow of chastity. He had sinned in the eyes of the church. But sex with Olivia was good.

It felt right. There was a definite energy that existed between them. Olivia was a kind, outgoing person, who was adventurous and anxious to please. She was more than just an available woman. In addition to being a firm believer in monogamy and a church goer, she was both intelligent and a listener. Her deceased father had been a Methodist minister and she believed in the sanctity of marriage and family. She had an amazing sense of humor and a sparkling smile. All these qualities combined to make her a 5' 5" sexy, feminine female. Evan was unsure if it was love, but whatever it was, he liked it. He liked it a lot.

The fact that Evan and Mac had not consummated their relationship gave Olivia hope that Evan might be the one. She had been lonely since the death of her husband and Evan was excellent company. He was also great in bed and anxious to please. Olivia hoped that a long-term relationship with Evan was in their future.

Over the next several weeks, Evan spent many cold winter nights with Olivia and his affection for her bloomed. Evan had told Mac about Olivia, but only of their friendship, not of their sexual relationship. Evan thought it best to keep that information to himself for the time being. Mac remained mostly distant from Evan, but since she had Precious for company, had become slightly more upbeat in Evan's presence. He remained hopeful that Mac would eventually recover from her depression and return to her old self. But right now he was in a bind. He wondered if it was possible to be in love with more than one woman at the same time. So what does a computer whiz do? Search social media, of course. After an extensive social media search, Evan then googled what the psychologists had to say. The consensus was that a man could love two or more women at the same time, but not equally. That was a major problem for Evan. He knew he loved both Olivia and Mac, but who was his favorite.

As winter became spring, Evan and Olivia's relationship continued to ripen. Mac and Fred were still in a state of depression, but improving. Then one spring day, Mac got a call from Scotland Yard. They had found and arrested the intruder who had fired the fatal shot killing Alice. He admitted to police in a plea deal that he had been paid by a Mexican drug lord, $5000 to disable Mac. It was the same drug kingpin who had threatened Mac on Mexican television for embarrassing his fiancée Maria at the French Open. The drug lord was currently in a Mexican prison serving 20 years for drug charges and money laundering. Finally, Mac and Fred had closure and Evan hoped the healing would begin.

A turning point happened 6 months later with a conversation involving Mac, Fred and Evan. Mac and Fred had been praying regularly about their future and in particular what Alice would want for the remaining portion of their lives. After weeks of prayer and soul-searching, they decided Alice would want two things; for Mac to pursue her dream of winning Wimbledon and for Evan and Mac to marry and have a family. Once that decision was made, Mac's attitude started to change and Evan felt improvement for her depression would soon follow. It did, but it was gradual. Mac started eating better and healthier. Dinner at the Appalachian Kitchen with Evan became a regular occurrence, but no tennis.

Playing in the Tygart River and fetching tennis balls were favorite activities of Precious. She was almost fully grown and Mac provided her with plenty of exercise. Exercise for Mac was not something she was ready to do, but Evan hoped that would come later. Mac was only 24 years of age and had time to get in tennis shape. But right now, she was a ghost of her former self with no interest in exercising.

Chapter 21

Evan continued to love both Olivia and Mac and patiently waited for Mac to return to her cheerful, former self. Mac was slowly becoming more available to Evan, both physically and emotionally and would often profess her love for Evan. However, she avoided talk about tennis and that made Evan uneasy. If Evan brought up the subject of tennis or Wimbledon, Mac would immediately shut down. This all changed when Evan, Mac and Precious were all on Mac's porch discussing world politics, when Mac suddenly said:

"I have an idea. I'm going to take Precious out to the clay court and throw her some tennis balls."

She then disappeared into the house and returned with a racquet and two tennis balls. The threesome then proceeded to the clay court where Mac began tossing tennis balls for Precious to retrieve. Evan sat on the courtside bench and watched. The tennis net had been stored in the nearby shed and the court had no obstructions except for the net posts. After a while Mac started hitting the balls with her racquet. This was what Evan had been waiting for. Mac was starting to think about tennis. Precious was making a mess of the clay court as she scurried about, chasing every tennis ball Mac hit.

Meanwhile, Evan's relationship with Olivia was fabulous and it was clear that Olivia was in love with him. On most every subject, Olivia was talkative and playful, except when the subject of Mac surfaced. Then she suddenly became quiet. Evan tried his best to stay clear of talking about Mac, but sometimes his feelings for Mac would surface.

During a pleasant dinner in Elkins, Evan was describing the previous day's activity with Precious and Mac. He was describing in great detail how Mac's lab was happily chasing this yellow tennis ball on the red clay of her tennis court, when a resolute Olivia suddenly interrupted.

"I can't take this anymore."
"What? Did I say something wrong?"
"Wrong? It's all wrong."
"What do you mean?"
"We can't be together for an evening without you talking about Mac and what she's doing or thinking."
"I'm sorry. I didn't mean…"
"If you're not talking about her, I'm sure you're thinking of her."
"That's not true. I love you and…"
"You love me? You may enjoy being in my bed, but I can't compete with your thoughts of her."

"That's not fair. Is there anything…?"

"Not really, because we're through. I've been thinking about this for a while now and I feel like I'm wasting my time. You may love me and love being with me, but I believe you love Mac more."

"How can you say that? You know I share a long history with Mac, but to say she is my favorite is crazy."

"Crazy or not, we're through."

"…Are you breaking up with me?"

"In a word. Yes."

Evan fell silent. He was speechless. He didn't know what to say. He knew his relationship with Olivia was special and he didn't want it to end. At least not like this. He studied Olivia's face to look for clues. He looked into her dark brown eyes and saw nothing but a blank stare. She was experiencing both heartache and humiliation and her luscious lips stiffened in an effort to hide her emotions. Sadly, he sensed that her mind was made up and there would be no turning back. On the car ride back to Mingo, an eerie silence penetrated the night's darkness. Evan walked Olivia to her door. They gave each other a brief hug and the date was over.

After the sudden breakup with Evan, Olivia entered into a period of emotional hibernation. Several months later she met a young wealthy banker from Webster Springs at a Catholic retreat in Elkins. He was of Hispanic heritage and they shared similar dreams of a future together. They fell madly in love and six months later they were married in a destination wedding in Costa Rica.

Meanwhile, Evan was crushed. He missed the energy and the vibe he had with Olivia. He knew loving two women was not sustainable, but the ending was so abrupt and final, he was an emotional wreck. It was a good time to lean on Mac and fortunately, she was receptive. Mac's improvement continued and she even started to exercise. When he could, Evan would join her, engaging in agility running, calisthenics and light stretching. In the beginning Evan could keep up with Mac, but in a few weeks Mac was improving so rapidly that Evan could no longer persist. He started watching more and exercising less, marveling at Mac's athleticism. Even Precious participated in some of the sprints. On the physical and emotional level, Mac was beginning to act like her old self. Her personality had been bruised, but she was regaining the identity that Evan had fallen in love with. They started spending more time together and romantic evenings in her two-bedroom cottage became frequent. Mac knew how to physically arouse Evan and she made sure that he was satisfied in a way that kept their shared vows of chastity intact.

One day while sipping an Earl Grey tea, Mac asked Evan an offbeat question:

"Would you like to hit some tennis balls?"
"Really? You know I'm not very good."
"It's okay. I suspect I'm not very good either."

Their expectation of not being very good, quickly became a reality. It clearly bothered Mac, but Evan was thrilled, because he knew this was a significant step forward in Mac's recovery. However, it didn't take long for Mac to replace Evan with the ball machine. She was physically still underweight, but her desire for perfection was apparent. Evan seemed to enjoy watching and Precious was mesmerized by the sheer number of bouncing tennis balls to chase.

The missing piece of this puzzle was Fred's depression. The love of his life and marriage partner for 35 years had been murdered and Fred struggled to maintain his sanity. For Mac's sake, he tried to hide his feelings, but losing the only woman he ever loved was hard and it weighed heavily on his every thought. Fred also had lost considerable weight and struggled constantly with bouts of anxiety. Nightmares were common and he had trouble focusing on routine tasks around the house. Fred was 55 years old and considered quite a catch among the 40-something women in the area, but Fred showed no interest in starting another romance.

While discussing grocery shopping with Fred, Mac emphasized that they both should try to eat healthier. After asking her dad if he would like to visit the Elkins Farmers Market and buy some locally-grown fruits and vegetables, Mac unexpectedly asked:

"Would you be willing to help me pursue one of mom's final requests?"
"Which one?"
"My dream of winning Wimbledon."
"You want me to help?"
"I need someone to travel with. I don't really feel safe travelling by myself."
"What about Evan?"
"Evan just received a promotion and is busy with his work."
"…I don't know if I could leave Harley and Charley."
"Dad, you've worked for them for almost 40 years. You do most of that work from home on your laptop and that can be done anywhere. I'm sure mom would want you to help. Please?"
"Well, I don't really like crowds."

"Oh Dad. It would be good for you."

"Maybe it would. I will talk with the brothers and see what they think."

"Okay and just so you know. I've decided to start my comeback at the Australian in 6 months, but I don't think I can do it without you being there."

"Sweetie, I hear you. Maybe it would be good for me."

A week later, Fred was all in and informed Mac that he would travel to Australia with her and do his best to cheer her on. The stage was set for Mac's comeback. The hard part lay ahead. Mac had been away from tennis for over two years. She was an underweight, out-of-shape woman with some serious work to do in order to get back to world-class tennis condition. It began with a call to Scott Flanagan to see if his invitation to train at his academy was still open. Scott was excited to hear Mac's voice and was surprised to hear that she wanted to return to world-class competition. He welcomed Mac with open arms to not only participate in his academy workouts, but offered her a fully-furnished two-bedroom apartment while training. Mac was eager to start and arranged for a 3-week training session to start next week.

Mac didn't realize how difficult it would be to get in competitive shape. For most of her life, Mac had been a world-class athlete and had never experienced a long period of inactivity. For the next six months, Mac did everything in her power to regain her former self. She ate right. She slept right and was obsessed with regaining her form. With the help of academy training sessions and Evan's unwavering support, Mac slowly improved. Mac was surprised by the number of young teen-age girls who could now beat her and it made her acutely aware of the increased depth of the women's field. Qualifiers

173

at major tournaments were no longer easy prey for main-draw players. This didn't discourage Mac, but only made her more determined to push forward.

Her main sponsors; Nike, Mercedes, Adidas, Rolex and Wilson had stayed with Mac in hopes of her return to the tour. Wilson was especially active in experimenting with Mac to find the best equipment for her style of play. The game had changed and Wilson wanted Mac to have the best racquet and strings to enhance her chances of a successful comeback.

The big day finally arrived and Mac and Fred were off to Australia. They flew to Honolulu, refueled and then flew to Melbourne. The total flight time was 25 hours. Once they arrived at the Grand Hyatt Melbourne Hotel, they were jet-lagged and took a much-needed nap. The next day, Mac took to the practice courts, which was a 5-minute ride or a 15-minute walk from the Grand Hyatt. She had no problem finding practice partners and most players were happy to see her back on the tour. Except for her practice sessions, Mac and Fred stayed mostly in their Diplomatic Suite and ordered room service. They enjoyed an expansive view of Melbourne and both felt relaxed before the tournament's start. Mac had a one-person security detail which was not really needed, since Mac was now old news and two teens from Ukraine were creating the majority of the media buzz.

For her first round match, Mac was assigned an outdoor show court which seated about 3000. The match was scheduled for 2 p.m. Australia time and the temperature was a warm 85°F. It was January but summer in Australia. During Mac's preparation in Charleston, the temperatures hovered near freezing and Mac had practiced primarily indoors in preparation. The standing-room-only crowd received Mac with a polite applause, but it was nothing compared to the raucous ovation given to her Australian opponent.

Mac got off to a quick start and won the first set in 50 minutes. During the second set, it was obvious that the heat was starting to bother Mac. At 3-2 in the second set, Mac started cramping and then became dizzy. Ten minutes later, Mac was forced to default due to an apparent heat stroke. The doctors on site measured her core body temperature to be 104°F. The extreme heat policy at the Australian Open (AO) was enforced an hour later and all outdoor matches were suspended.

Mac's quest for a title at the AO was over. With rest and some serious hydration, Mac was able to mostly recover three days later. Mac was disappointed but not discouraged. She would learn from this and was already developing a plan to acclimate to the heat. Next year she would arrive 3 weeks early and play some much-needed warm-up tournaments down under. She also made note of the heavier Dunlop balls that are used in the AO. She made a mental note to practice accordingly next year.

Mac was eager to return home and begin preparations for the French Open. She had been in phone contact every day with Evan and was anxious to return and share some quality time. Fred wanted to stay and do some sightseeing. It was their first time in Australia and Fred thought it would do them both good to explore Melbourne and maybe fly to New Zealand.

"Why don't we stay an additional two weeks and see some of the sights of Melbourne?"
"Oh, Dad. I'm tired. I would rather go home."

"I think we would be wasting a good opportunity. It took us a long time to get here and our contract with our two pilots runs another two weeks. We could rent a car and start with the Hanging Rock Reserve. It's only about 50 miles from downtown Melbourne and I hear they have an excellent café right below the Hanging Rocks. We could even give our security guard some time off."

"I really don't want to."

"Honey, I believe it would do us both good. We could do some exploring and share a new adventure."

"...Well, if you really want to. Okay."

The next day they rented a 5-speed manual transmission SUV. Having the steering wheel on the right and the gear shift on the left took some getting used to, but after driving for about 30 minutes and negotiating a couple of roundabouts, Fred was comfortable driving. Their first adventure was the Hanging Rock Reserve where they enjoyed a blueberry scone and cappuccino on the Café patio. The next day, the weather was perfect and they decided to take a drive on the Great Ocean Road. So began one week of exploring the sights around Melbourne

Their next stop was Hobart, Tasmania. The flight time from Melbourne was 1 hour and 15 minutes. Once at the airport and after another SUV rental, they were off to the Sorell Fruit Farm. It was only 11 kilometers (6.8 miles) from the airport and they arrived in time for a morning snack of strawberry croissants and cappuccinos. They even bought a quart of fresh-picked cherries to snack on that evening. The second day was spent at the Bonorong Wildlife Sanctuary, where they were able to see the nearly-extinct Tasmanian devil plus a multitude of kangaroos. Mac enjoyed petting several of the friendlier marsupials who always seemed ready for the next snack. Even Fred marveled at the many animals on display during this once-in-a-lifetime experience.

Two days on the island of Tasmania were followed by a 3-hour flight to Auckland, New Zealand (NZ). Once there and another rental, they were off to see snow-capped mountain peaks and magnificent waterfalls. They especially enjoyed the friendliness of the NZ people. The *Maori* spirit of *Manaakitanga* (hospitality and generosity) is a tradition still relevant today on this magical island nation.

Soon it was time to make the 25 hour flight trip back to WV and share with Evan some of their recently-discovered adventures.

Chapter 22

After a long flight from Auckland, Fred and Mac were met at the Elkins Airport by Evan. He was overjoyed to see Mac and was anxious to hear of their adventures. On the way back to Valley Head, Mac and Fred gave Evan a play-by-play on their travels down under. Fred was partial to the Sorell Fruit Farm and the Bonorong Wildlife Sanctuary, while Mac's favorites were the waterfalls and mountain peaks of NZ.

It was a little over 4 months until the French Open and Mac still had a lot of work to do in order to improve her physical condition and to sharpen her tennis skills. Mac's clay court had been repaired and groomed during Mac's absence and she started in earnest to continue her comeback. Her relationship with Evan was still strong and they saw each other almost every night when she was in Valley Head. Mac had regained her lost weight and her curves that had been lost during her period of depression. In order to compete against world-class competition, her aerobic conditioning and flexibility needed some serious improvement. During her Australia trip, Mac's personality had improved and although she had been scarred due to her mother's death, she had regained some of her charismatic personality. However, she was still guarded in sharing her feelings, overly cautious, and less confident in her athletic abilities. However, her resolve to win Wimbledon was as resolute as ever.

While in Valley Head, Mac practiced daily on her clay court, using the ball machine and serving 200 serves a day (100 righty and 100 lefty). Wind sprints, agility running and yoga-style stretching were regular parts of her day. She spent two 3-week training blocks at the Flanagan Tennis Academy where she fared better when playing the top players. She still planned no warm-up tournaments before Paris and was convinced she was in the best shape of her life. She felt ready to compete at Roland Garros.

Mac and Evan remained fully committed to each other and planned to be married once Mac had achieved her dream and retired from the tour. Evan knew he couldn't keep his past sexual relationship with Olivia a secret forever. He needed to confess before they were married, but was rightly concerned as to when would be the right time and he knew now was not it. He judged that Mac would be upset when she heard his confession, but prayed that Mac would forgive him for betraying her trust. He prayed upon this regularly, but his religious upbringing would not allow him to hide this lie forever from the one he loved. The thought of revealing this transgression was a constant worry.

As Fred and Mac left for Paris, Mac felt she was ready to start winning on the world stage. They arrived three days early and Mac's practice sessions went well. She was given a direct entry into the main draw and was paired against the top-ranked French player in the first round. They were paired on an outdoor show court. The temperature was a mild sunny 60°F and windy. Mac was nervous before the match, during the match and played poorly in losing in straight sets. She did not handle her nerves, the wind or her opponent. In a nutshell, her confidence had been shattered. The partisan French crowd didn't help much, since they were in a celebratory mood and seemed to barely acknowledge the dejected Mac.

Fred and a miserable Mac immediately left Paris and journeyed home. Fred tried to comfort Mac, but to no avail. Fred had never seen Mac play that bad, but didn't say much about it, fearing his comments would only make matters worse.

When they arrived back in WV, they were greeted by Evan and a tearful Mac melted into Evan's arms. Through tears and sobs, she whispered to him:

"I played so bad."
"It's okay. You'll do better the next time."
"I don't know if there will be a next time."
"What do you mean?"
"I think I may quit."
"Mac, you're not a quitter."
"I think I've lost my ability to compete."

After a few days back in Valley Head, Mac and Fred had a heart-to-heart discussion about continuing on the tour. Fred pointed out that she had experienced disappointment before but had always bounced back stronger. He also reminded Mac that this is not how your mother would want your tennis to end.

"I know dad, but this is different. I have lost all confidence in myself."
"Confidence can be regained. A couple of good matches and it should return."
"Maybe, but…"
"Think about it for a few days."
"I will."
"A call to Scott Flanagan might help"
"Okay, I will text him tomorrow."

The next day Scott called Mac and they did some serious face time.

"Scott, I've lost my confidence."
"How so?"
"I get nervous when I play. I have this fear I can't beat anybody."
"Anything else?"
"I have this fear that I will let everyone down if I lose. You are the only coach I have ever known. Can you help?"
"I might, if you are willing to help yourself."
"Okay, what do I do?"
"First, you will have to train your subconscious mind by engaging in positive self-talk the evening before every match. You will need to visualize the match as vividly as you can. You want to imagine that you are making all your shots consistently, without errors. You then visualize hitting that last winner on match point, shaking your opponent's hand and hearing the cheers of the crowd after you've won."

"Okay, I can do that."

"Next, you will need to lower your expectations and play only for your own enjoyment, not for anyone else; not for Fred; not for Evan or your revered mother."

"Okay."

"Next, you will need to play in the present and forget past mistakes and missed opportunities. And you must avoid thinking of the future. I think it would be helpful to practice singing the lyrics to the famous *song Que Sera, Sera. Whatever will be will be? The future's not ours to see…* "

"I know the song well. Anything else?"

"Write these ideas on a note card and if needed, refer to them during a match."

"I will try."

"Don't try. Just do it and good luck."

"Thanks, Scott. I will let you know of any improvement."

Before heading off to London and the Wimbledon Championships, Mac mentally practiced Scott's ideas every day. She regularly sang the song *Que Sera, Sera* and memorized the lyrics. Because she was a former French Open Champion, Mac did get an invite to play in the Boodles exhibition prior to Wimbledon.

Mac was accepted directly into the main draw based on her protected ranking and drew a tricky veteran in the first round. Mild temperatures and no wind made for ideal conditions and Mac was eager to just enjoy the match. Mac got off to a fast start and won 6-3, 6-3 in just over an hour. The half-filled stadium crowd cheered for Mac, but not like before. People have short memories and the Wimbledon crowd was no exception. Mac's next opponent was a qualifier, who had won in three sets in her previous match and this was her first time in the second round of a major. Mac made the rookie mistake of looking forward to her projected next match against a seeded player. Mac may have disregarded the lyrics; ...*the future's not ours to see...* Mac was caught looking ahead before she had won in the present. Her young opponent played well and beat Mac 6-4, 6-4 in 90 minutes. Mac was shocked but realized too late that focusing on the future does not win matches in the present. Mac was out of Wimbledon and she and Fred were headed back to WV.

Back in Valley Head, Mac called Scott and told him about her tournament. She had taken her opponent for granted and told Scott she would not make that mistake again. Despite her disappointment at Wimbledon, Mac planned to continue with her planned schedule. Her next tournament would be the US Open.

Chapter 23

At the US Open, Mac started strong and to her surprise, won her first four matches in straight sets. She was playing like the old Mac. The day before the quarter-finals, Mac and Fred were having lunch at the Tavern on the Green. This iconic eatery is located on the west side of Central Park and is a legendary eating place for the well-heeled of NY. While eating her chopped vegetable salad, Mac noticed Fred staring at an adjacent table.

"Dad, at what are you staring?"
"Nothing, really."
"It looks like you staring at those two women to your right."

A moment later a petite middle-aged woman approached their table and asked Mac.

"Are you Mackenzie, the tennis player from WV?"

"Yes, I am. Who's asking?"

"My name is Anna Johnson and I've been a big fan of yours for several years. When you play in NY, I always try to watch your matches."

"Are you from WV?"

"Yes, I am. I live in Wheeling and I'm an environmental lawyer with the firm Johnson, Sweeney and Brown."

"Well. It's nice to meet a fellow West Virginian and a protector of our environment."

Fred was smitten by this petite lady from Wheeling. He guessed her to be about 40 and he liked what he saw. He hadn't paid much attention to any woman since Alice's death, but this petite doll was different. To Mac's surprise, Fred, at long last, blurted out.

"I'm Mac's dad and my name is Fred. Would you and your friend like to join us?"

"I'll ask my friend."

As she motioned to her friend. Fred arose like a gentleman should. Once the four were seated, the conversation was like a tennis match. The conversation bounced back and forth on the subjects of tennis and the environment. Their discussion was delightful and eventually Mac invited them to join Fred in her player's box. She had empty seats and felt comfortable in asking.

"Would you like to join my dad in my player's box tomorrow? If that's okay with you, dad?"

185

"Of course, that would be great. I could sure use the company."

"Wow, we would be thrilled. Our seats are in the nose-bleed section and to sit in Mac's player box would be a dream come true."

The next day Mac found herself in a tense 3-set struggle and despite the enthusiastic cheering from her player's box, Mac finished a close second. She competed well, but was ultimately outplayed by an up-and-coming Czech player, losing the third set tiebreaker 12-10. Having concluded her calendar-year schedule, Mac immediately began preparation for her trip down under. She was finally enjoying the process of improving and was less focused on her results.

Once back in Valley Head, Fred began a whirlwind romance with the lawyer from Wheeling, and Mac's love affair with Evan showed no signs of cooling.

Mac now looked forward to a well-deserved rest before the long trip down under to the AO. Her sponsors were excited and promotional appearances were many. As Mac was regaining her previous form, Evan was just happy to see a major improvement in Mac's personality.

It was soon time to make the long trip to the Australian. This time Mac decided to play some warm-up tournaments before the AO. She hoped to acclimate to the heat. Mac's first event was the Brisbane International, which takes place on the east coast in Queensland located in what's known as the Gold Coast. The region gets its name from the pricey homes located along the beach just south of Brisbane. The tournament is a combined WTA and ATP event and is one of the few tournaments where the women's prize money is significantly larger than the men's. The women's draw was 64 players with a top singles' prize of $250,000 (US) and the men's had 32 players with a top prize of $100,000 (US). The event is a WTA 500 and the men's is an ATP 250. Since the Brisbane International begins in late December, Mac and Fred left on Christmas Day, and arrived 4 days before the start of the tournament. Mac played reasonable well, but wilted in the extreme heat and lost in the second round.

At Hobart, she fared somewhat better but lost in the quarters. Mac was satisfied with how she played and handled the summer conditions. Now it was on to Melbourne and the AO.

Wearing a gorgeous all-white Adidas outfit with a matching white hat, she felt ready to compete. She made sure to apply a liberal amount of sunscreen if playing outdoors. Mac was seeded #20 and surgically breezed through her first two rounds. Playing the #2 seed in the round of 32, she was again unlucky. She was scheduled to play on an outdoor court at 2 p.m. Her opponent was a former AO champion, who dealt with the windy, hot, outdoor conditions better than Mac. She lost a tough three setter, but played reasonably well, considering the circumstances.

After the long flight back home, Mac wondered if there was any additional conditioning she could do to better prepare. She discussed this conditioning dilemma with Scott, who had no additional advice for the AO, but did say that staying injury free was the most important thing. He cautioned against over training and felt she had just been unlucky. Scott assured her that her fortune would eventually change. Mac was obviously playing better and was advised to just stay the course. The four-month break after her trip down under gave Mac an opportunity to continue her mental and physical improvement. The French Open would begin in June and she was going to make sure she was ready.

The French fans were happy to see Mac, who won three close matches before losing in the fourth round. Fred and Mac stayed in Paris for a week and then it was on to London. She played well at Wimbledon, but took a disappointing loss in the third round to the defending Wimbledon Champion. Mac had handled the tricky grass surface much better and was pleased with that part of her progress.

Mac was physically and mentally tired after Wimbledon and decided to skip the US Open for some needed rest. She would begin the New Year in Australia.

Chapter 24

It was mid-September and the vibrant colors of fall were on full display. WV is a special place to observe the color change of their abundant mountain forests. It is the only state that is located entirely within the Appalachian Mountain region and the assortment of burnt orange, crisp red and bright yellow hues form a memorable sight that is a must-see experience. But Fred's mind was elsewhere and focused on another experience. He had arranged for a first date with Anna and he was on his way to Wheeling. He had washed and detailed his new truck and was ready for the 3 ½ hour drive north. Since both he and Anna liked Italian food, Fred had made reservations at the highly-recommended restaurant Figaretti's and was anxious to learn more about Anna. Fred arrived at her door promptly at 7:30 and he was not disappointed. Anna was a knockout and Fred felt she could be that special one. On the trip to Figaretti's, Anna was a talkative seductive beauty, who even laughed at Fred's lame jokes. Fred was a good listener and liked what he heard.

"Fred, tell me about yourself."
"There's not much to tell really; my claim to fame is being Mac's dad."
"Are you employed?"
"I do the financials for an auto repair business in Valley Head and I handle Mac's travel schedule, negotiate her sponsor deals and accompany her while she's on tour."
"Now you're trying to impress me."
"Did it work?"
"Maybe… I'm hoping you're unattached."
"I am."
"I'm sure you must miss your wife."
"I do; bless her soul. She was my first and only love. We met in high school and were married for 37 years."

Anna had read the accounts of his wife's killing, but was hoping he was dating no one special. Fred was so busy answering questions, he hadn't had time to really study Anna, but he like everything he saw. Her large brown eyes, glistening in the restaurant's soft lighting, matched perfectly with her smooth olive skin and delicate features. Silky black hair fell just below her shoulders and in Fred's view, she was a goddess.

"Anna, tell me about you."
"I grew up in Italy and migrated to the U.S. when I was six. I come from a family of lawyers and my late husband was a lawyer."
"What ever happened to your husband?"

"He was killed in a head-on collision returning from a client meeting in Webster Springs."

"I'm so sorry. It must have been devastating."

"It was. It happened three years ago and he was killed instantly. I would rather talk about something else, if you don't mind."

"Okay, what is your favorite Italian food?"

"Lasagna, of course."

"Have you ever visited Italy?"

"I've been back only once; about 10 years ago. Have you been?"

"No, I haven't. Mac has talked about playing the Italian Open, but it's just been talk."

"You should go. I think you would like it."

"Maybe I will. It's only fair for me to ask. Are you dating anyone?"

"No, but I might be tempted by the right person."

Anna's plump, luscious lips gradually broke into a subtle smile as she pondered her growing attraction to Fred. He was a square-jawed well-preserved man, who had a certain vibe that she found engaging. Anna wondered if he might be ready for romance.

After dinner, the conversation in Fred's truck was friendly, but uneventful. After walking Anna to her door, she invited Fred in for a nightcap.

"Would you like to come in for a refreshment?"

"Well, I don't drink alcohol, but a cup of coffee might be nice."

"Okay, I will make us some coffee."

Later in the evening, Fred was ready to start back to Valley Head. It was after midnight and Anna worried that driving on the mountain roads at night would be too dangerous. The vision of her ex-husband's accident still haunted her.

"Fred, why don't you spend the night here and drive back in the morning? I do have a spare bedroom and bath."
"I don't want to impose."
"Nonsense. Follow me."

Once settled in a king-size bed for the night, Fred was dreaming of Anna. Unbeknownst to Fred, Anna had quietly entered Fred's room and slipped under the covers. Fred was slowly stirred from his slumber by the soft scent of perfume. He wasn't sure if he was dreaming or if this was real. Either way, he was enjoying the ride and what a ride it was. Sometime later, the merger of two lonely souls was consummated. During the remainder of the night, built-up physical tensions and raw emotions were swept away and the morning brought a certain tranquility to both Fred and Anna.

Thus began a whirl-wind romance, with magical evenings and some serious, but scenic driving. Fred and Anna were a happy couple and even though they came from very different backgrounds, the attraction they felt for each other was undeniable.

As Mac's confidence and results improved, Evan and Mac continued to draw closer. Their inseparability was marred only by Mac's 3-week training sessions at The Scott Flanagan Tennis Academy. Even when Mac was training, Evan would make the 3-hour drive to Charleston to spend enjoyable weekends with Mac.

Chapter 25

$\mathcal{F}$inally, the time arrived to take the 25-hour flight to Australia. This time they would leave the day after Christmas, so that Mac could again play the two warm-up tournaments before the first Slam of the year. Anna and Evan were both at the Elkins Airport to see them off. After multiple hugs and kisses, Mac and Fred were off to Hawaii and then Brisbane.

In Brisbane, Mac practiced with a young player from Dayton, OH, who asked Mac if she would like to play doubles. Since Mac was trying to acclimate to the conditions, she thought it might be a good idea and agreed. Her name was Allison McFarland and she had long blond hair, green eyes and pale white skin. She was about the same height and build as Mac, but only 18 years old. Allison's singles ranking was #150, and they both were accepted into the main draw in singles and doubles. To Mac's surprise, she won the singles and won the doubles with Allison. They got along famously and Mac enjoyed the doubles so much, she asked Allison if she would like to play doubles in Hobart the following week. Mac even offered to fly Allie and her coach John, to Tasmania in her private jet; a trip of approximately 3 hours.

Mac, Fred, Allie, John, 2 pilots and one security person (7 people in all) were on their way to Hobart. Allie viewed Mac as a mentor and took in all the advice Mac gave her. It was Allie's first time down under and she was all ears. She listened closely as Mac strongly recommended sunscreen, all white clothes and a white hat. The summer sun in Australia was tough and Mac made Allie well aware of its strength.

Mac won the singles in Hobart and she and Allie easily won the doubles. Mac was a tiger at net and they had a marvelous time together. Next it was on to Melbourne and Mac again offered Allie and her coach a ride on her jet. Mac knew that the AO would be a different ball game with all the top-ranked players scheduled to participate. Being somewhat superstitious, Mac and Allie decided to enter both the singles and doubles again, thinking that might continue their good fortune.

Once the AO was underway, Allie drew a seeded opponent and lost in the first round. Mac won a late evening match on Rod Laver Arena in straight sets and avoided the feared Aussie heat. Since Mac's next 5 singles' matches were all in prime time at night, she received a reprieve from Australia's searing summer temperatures. The finals began at 2 p.m. and the temperature was uncommonly mild but windy. Mac handled the wind better than her opponent and won 7-5 in the third set. The partisan crowd cheered wildly for Mac during the trophy presentation. Mac was all smiles as she predictably praised her opponent and the crowd. Mac and Allie again dominated the doubles and won their 3rd straight tournament. This was the 2nd singles' Slam that Mac had won; one French and one AO.

Scott sent Mac a text soon after the finals and declared that her luck must have changed. After fulfilling several sponsor commitments in Australia, Mac, Fred, Allie and her coach, along with both pilots promptly made the 25-hour flight back to WV. They were jubilantly met at the Elkins Airport by Evan, Anna and Allie's family. Mac's remaining schedule for the year would be challenging, and she looked forward to some much needed rest. Indian Wells, Miami, Roland Garros, Wimbledon and the US Open would round out the rest of her year.

Mac stayed away from tennis during the month of February and focused her energy on Pilates and flexibility. She had taken the suggestion of Scott seriously and made every effort to remain injury free. The harsh winter was still very much evident in the hills of WV, but Mac's future plans were anything but harsh. Her mental outlook and physical appearance had improved so much that Evan felt certain that Mac had returned as the person he knew and loved. Mac pondered her future after tennis and she was certain that Evan was a big part of that future.

While planning her dinner date with Evan, Mac asked her dad if he and Anna would like to join them for dinner at the Al Dente Ristorante in the Snowshoe Mountain Lodge. Mac and Evan had never eaten there before and Mac knew her dad and Anna liked Italian food, so it seemed like a natural fit. The only problem was the roads. Fred's truck was able to navigate the

WV mountain roads easily in snowy conditions, but a trip from Wheeling in Anna's' Honda might pose an unnecessary risk. Fred came up with a solution. He would drive his truck to Wheeling, spend the night there and then drive back with Anna the following day. They could then be ready for dinner that evening. Accordingly, reservations were made for four on a Saturday night and all involved hoped for good weather. When a major snow storm developed on Saturday, their plans appeared snowed under.

But Anna saved the evening by offering to cook an authentic Italian dinner. She was able to find enough ingredients in Fred's kitchen to create a savory meal of minestrone soup and pasta pomodora. The two men eagerly devoured the meal and Mac thought it was so good, she asked for the recipe. After dinner, the flickering flames of Fred's fireplace creation was the ideal setting for the evening's conversation. With a back log anchoring twinkling embers, the small talk lasted well into the evening.

The next morning, Mac was ready for some tennis, but the weather was not. It would be another week before Mac's Valley Head clay court would be ready for play. She texted Scott and inquired about a spot at his Academy for a 3-week training session. Charleston still had snow on the ground, so some training might have to be indoors. A March training session was arranged and she and Evan were off to Charleston.

After three weeks at Scott's Academy, Mac returned to Valley Head and her well-maintained hard court. Mac, her ball machine and Precious began final preparations for Indian Wells. Mac had always played well on hard courts and looked forward to a return to Indian Wells. In singles, she had won two major titles; one French Open and one Australian.

In late March, Mac and Fred were off to Palm Springs. Mac was now ranked #8 in the world and was seeded #4. She and Allison were entered in the doubles and seeded eighth. Allison had cracked the top 100 and gained direct entry into the main draw. Before the tournament's start, Mac and Allison spent three days practicing on the hard courts of Indian Wells. They both felt ready and were eager to start. Mac won the singles and doubles with Allison. Allison won two singles matches.

It was then off to Miami where Mac again won the singles and doubles with Allison. Mac's spotless singles record for the year was 31-0. Improving with every tournament, Allison won 3 matches.

After a two-month break, it was off to Paris and The French Open. Mac and Allison both won first round matches in both singles and doubles. In the second round Allison lost a tough 3-setter to a seeded player and Mac continued her winning streak. Afterwards everything went well for Mac until the semifinals of the singles. It had rained all day in Paris and Mac's match was started and stopped several times before the roof was closed on Court Philippe Chatrier. Once play resumed, the clay court was still moist and Mac was struggling to find her footing. She was half-way through the third set, when she starting having flash-backs of her head-first collision with the umpire stand several years earlier. While seated during the break, she retrieved her note cards detailing focusing tips from Scott. One tip stood out. *Forget the past. Play in the present.* These words were enough to shift Mac's focus. She would go on to win the next three games to close out a tense semi-final. In the singles final, Mac played flawlessly and prevailed in straight sets. Mac had now won two French Open singles' titles and remained undefeated for the year. She and Allison also won the doubles to make a statement that reverberated throughout the tennis community. Mac would enter next month's Wimbledon as the #1 seed and ranked #1 by the WTA. She and Allison would be the #1seed in doubles.

Mac was again on top of the tennis world. Paparazzi and autograph seekers were everywhere. Security was tight, but Mac's focus was elsewhere. She was now ready to achieve her dream of winning Wimbledon. She took advantage of her Boodles invitation and had some splendid practices on grass. Because only the top 25 men and women were invited, practicing with Allison was not an option. Mac was clearly the number one option with the wealthy male patrons and even Fred gathered some attention from the ladies.

Meanwhile, over at the Eastbourne International, Allison was gaining her own fans. Gentlemen admirers flocked to gain a glimpse of this rising young beauty. Considering that it was her first grass court event, Allison played well at Eastbourne losing a close match in the quarter-finals.

During Wimbledon, Mac, Fred, Allison and her coach opted to stay at the luxurious Hilton Biltmore Mayfair Hotel. They booked the Lord Harrowby Suite which gave everyone plenty of room. With the exception of their practice sessions, Mac and Allison stayed mostly in their suite where security was less complicated and the room service superb. All four got along famously and Allison looked forward to playing both the singles and the doubles. However, Mac was conflicted.

On the outside, Mac appeared to be a pillar of confidence. Someone who was at the height of her tennis powers and a heavy favorite to win the prestigious Wimbledon title. She had won two straight Slam titles. She boasted a spotless won-lost record of 38-0, was seeded #1 and was undefeated for the first half of the year. She was injury free and healthy. So, what could possibly go wrong? In Mac's mind, a lot of things. Mac was experiencing a severe case of anxiety. This became evident when Mac and Allison were discussing their first round opponents, the night before the start of Wimbledon. Mac startled Allison by admitting:

"Allie, for some reason I have the jitters."
"Why?"
"I don't know. I normally don't get nervous before matches."
"Why is this different?"
"I'm losing my confidence."
"Mac, over the last 6 months, you have been hands down the best player in the world."
"I know my record is good, but the expectations people have is starting to weigh on me. I've also lost my note card of tips from my coach…"
"Just send him a text and ask him to give you some reminders."
"Okay, I will do that now."

Later, Mac made her daily call to Evan. It was 8 p.m. in London and 1 a.m. in Valley Head. Evan was wide awake and always looked forward to his conversations with Mac. Mac's voice sounded conflicted when she stammered:

"Evan, I'm getting nervous thinking about tomorrow."

"Why, sweetheart?"

"I'm not sure. I've had bouts of nerves in the past, but there was always a good reason?"

"You've been playing great. Do you have an injury?"

"No, but the expectations people have is starting to…"

"You'll be okay. Just remember what Scott told you the last time you were having an issue with your confidence."

She sobbed as her voice elevated. "This is my big chance Evan: It's what I've always dreamed of and now I'm doubting myself. I've even lost my note cards and…"

For the next hour Mac released a torrent of intense emotion and recalled all the hurdles that had impeded her path to tennis celebrity. Mac recounted her heat stroke at the AO; the concussion at Roland Garros; the machete attack at the US Open and her mother's death at Wimbledon. Their conversation stayed strained until the call finally ended with each professing their love for one another. That night Mac slept very little. She had multiple nightmares about her mother's death and a fear of the future.

Mac's first match was on Centre Court, and as she walked through the newly renovated entrance, she again made note of the famous quote of Rudyard Kipling. . "If you can meet with triumph and disaster and treat those two imposters just the same…" Mac had experienced the life-changing death of her mother, but could she now triumph. How could she treat these two imposters the same? The new entrance led players underneath the Royal Box and directly onto Centre Court. Mac slowly walked on wobbly legs toward the player's bench. She was a nervous wreck. Mac received a thunderous round of applause from the mostly English spectators as the sold-out stadium anticipated a grandiose display of tennis. The crowd was behind Mac one-hundred percent. However, her first round opponent was a wily veteran who had played at Wimbledon many times and seemed unfazed by the enthusiasm of the partisan crowd.

Mac got off to a shaky start and lost the first set quickly 6-0. The crowd was stunned. There were very few points to applaud. The play from Mac was uncharacteristically sloppy and Mac was on the verge of defeat. On a change-over, deep in the second set, Mac received a long-awaited text from Scott. His words seemed to spark a resurgence in Mac and the crowd began to respond. As Mac began to settle down, the aggressive play of this wily veteran turned a little more conservative. The thought of upending the world's #1 was too much and Mac finally prevailed; 0-6, 7-5 and 6-2. Later that day, she and Allison won their doubles match in straight sets. Mac was through to the second round in both singles and doubles and could finally relax.

On day three, Mac drew an experienced Ukrainian player in the second round, who had recently returned to the tour after rehabbing a hip injury. Mac's anxiety had improved, but she was still tense. The prime time evening match was uneventful until Mac developed a cramp in her right hand. The announcers believed it to be tension cramps that can develop because of nerves. Fortunately, because of her ambidextrous style, Mac was able to finish the match playing left-handed. The final score was 7-5 and 7-5 and she was in the third round. Mac and Allison continued their winning streak in doubles and advanced.

On day five, Mac was feeling more confident and playing better. She was playing a well-known Russian player, when a light drizzle began during the first set. The roof was then closed, but when play resumed the court was still slippery. Her Russian opponent refused to play because of the conditions, but after discussions with officials, players were ordered to continue. Once play continued, Mac took a nasty fall on the damp grass and arose to her feet limping. After a medical timeout, a taped ankle and a bandage over an elbow scrape, play continued. Mac moved gingerly, but was able to serve well enough to advance to the next round. Allison and Mac again won their doubles with Allison dominating play.

On day seven, Mac and Allison both won their fourth round singles matches. It wasn't until that evening that they found out they would play each other in the quarter-finals. It would be their first time playing each other in a tournament and both were uneasy about the encounter. Mac and Allison were best friends and this would be a bona fide test of their friendship. Allison was a hard-hitting left-hander, who had improved immensely in the last six months. Her WTA ranking had risen from #150 to #45 and she was constantly benefiting from Mac's mentorship.

Day nine finally arrived and Mac and Allison were scheduled for a prime-time night match. They both were in good shape physically, but mentally, it was a different story. This was a huge match for both players and for different reasons. They had their mental demons to deal with and both were conflicted. Allison's coach had brilliantly prepared her to take on Mac. John knew Mac's strengths and weaknesses and had developed the perfect plan to dethrone the world's top player. The sold-out arena cheered loudly as they entered Centre Court. Allison had her share of supporters, but Mac remained the crowd favorite. The match was a brilliant display of power tennis and the difference between them was one or two crucial points. But in the end, Mac won a brilliant 3-hour match in three sets. The match culminated with both players sharing a warm embrace. In the post-match press conference, both gave high praise to each other. There were no hard feelings between Mac and Allison. The most disappointed person was likely Allison's coach, but even he was pleased with how well Allison had played. He seemed confident that his charge would have many more chances for major titles. The next day Mac and Allison demolished their hapless opponents in less than an hour.

On day 11, Mac's semi-final opponent was her junior nemesis Emma. The media was hyping this as a must see match of the tournament. Considering their history beginning as 12-year-olds, Mac had good reason to be apprehensive. Emma was a seasoned veteran and the #3 seed. The memory of her mother's killing before the Wimbledon final was still a vivid memory. Mac knew this would be a difficult match physically and mentally and she prepared herself accordingly. It was a prime-time night match under starry skies with no wind and an open roof.

As Mac entered the sold-out stadium, she was greeted with deafening standing ovation. Even the royal box was standing. Mac acknowledged the greeting with her trademark radiant smile and was ready to play the best tennis of her life. However, Emma and her coach had also been preparing for this day, and Emma was on fire. The backcourt exchanges produced highlight reels, with both players playing with the slimmest of margins. Two tennis champions in the prime of their tennis life were giving the fans an extraordinary display of grass-court tennis. Roaring applause punctuated almost every point as the crowd began cheering for both players. On this evening, and by the slimmest of margins, Mac proved to be the better player. She outlasted Emma in three electric sets. After Mac and Emma embraced warmly at the net, the crowd erupted with a standing ovation for both players. The meeting with the press was unusual, because both Emma and Mac sat before the press to answer their questions. There were no losers or tears. With their arms draped over each other's shoulders, they appeared the best of friends. They thanked everyone they could think of, and marveled at the energy of the crowd. Accolades were heaped on each other with reckless abandon and nothing but joy permeated the newsroom.

The following day Mac and Allison again dominated in their doubles. Allison seemed to be improving with every match and Mac is no longer surprised by Allison's sterling play.

Chapter 26

$\mathcal{T}$he big day had finally arrived. Evan had purchased a one-way ticket to London to support Mac and was probably more nervous than she was. Mac was one step away from achieving her dream. She had spent a sleepless night trying to disperse the demons that haunted her. Mac would have Evan, Fred, Allison and coach in her player's box. Scott, Jim and Anna were all watching in WV.

Her opponent was born and raised in the Southwest (SW) portion of London adjoining the grounds of Wimbledon. In fact, Wimbledon is sometimes referred to as SW19, where the 19 refers to the area's postal code. Lucy was raised in the (SW) region of London with a postal code of 18. Her name was Lucy Armstrong and she was a lanky, left-handed grass-court specialist, who had attended numerous Championships as a young child and at one time served as a ball girl. Like Mac, she was a tennis prodigy, who had won the Wimbledon Junior Championships as a 16-year-old. She had received a wild card into Wimbledon and was on a 14 match win streak. Lucy had enjoyed the benefit of the best British coaches from the time she was six and had honed her game on grass. Lucy had received major financial support from the Lawn Tennis Association (LTA) and moral support from her *mum* and dad. Her parents were both first-rate amateur players, who had introduced their daughter to tennis at an early age. Wimbledon's last Women's Champion was Virginia Wade, who won the singles in 1977 and the English fans were hungry for another.

On the other side of the net was MacKenzie Hamrick, who had grown up in the hills of WV, with no financial support from the USTA and a moderate amount of coaching from Scott Flanagan. Starting tennis at age six, her primary practice partner was her uncle's barn door.

As the players emerged from under the Royal Box, the applause was deafening. Understandably, Mac was extremely nervous and not feeling her best; either mentally or physically. However, the bookies in London had made Mac a heavy favorite. After all, she was the number one player in the world. She had won four Slam titles. She was undefeated for the year and on a 38 match win streak. Why would you bet against her?

The Royal Box included Prince William, Kate and their three children. But the Royal Box was no ordinary Box. Royalty and celebrities were numerous and included: The Duchess of Cambridge; King Philip VI of Spain; Daniel Craig and his wife;

former Wimbledon Champions, Billie Jean King and Stan Smith; Tim Davie, the chairman of Rolex.

The limit of one thousand fans jockeyed for position on Henman Hill to watch the match on big screen TVs and thousands of Brits tuned to their household *telly* to watch the match live.

Mac quickly realized that this match would be different and require her to focus like never before. The crowd, which had been behind Mac the entirety of the tournament, was now understandably behind Lucy. Mac started slowly, while Lucy, with nothing to lose, was playing with reckless abandon. Every time Lucy would hit a winner, the crowd would go nuts. When Mac hit an amazing shot, polite applause and Mac's box supplied the only source of recognition. Lucy won the first set and then Mac started playing better in the second. The crowd was in a frenzy and every game was a war of attrition. Mac pulled out the second set and they were on to a third. Lucy took a 9-minute bathroom break after the second set, while Mac nervously practiced her serve on court. The third set was a masterpiece of power tennis with each player displaying remarkable athleticism and a refusal to lose. Lucy faltered slightly at the match's most critical times and Mac vanquished the last of her demons to win her third major of the year.

After finishing the match with an ace, Mac fell to her knees, bent down and kissed the grass. When she arose, she pointed to the heavens and mouthed the words; *for you mom.* The spectators gave both players a standing ovation as they embraced at the net. Evan climbed down from Mac's box and rushed past security to give Mac a long hug and kiss. Allison was hugging everyone she could find. Mac was presented the Venus Rosewater Dish, presented by the Duchess of

Cambridge (Kate Middleton). The dish is a sterling silver salver that is partially gilded. It is 44.5 cm (1 ½ ft) in diameter and weighed 3.5 kg (7.3 lbs.). What is now the current tradition, Mac proudly walked around Centre Court, holding the plate high over her head for all to see. Mac beamed her radiant smile, knowing that she had finally realized the dream of a 6-year-old girl from Valley Head. In her acceptance speech, Mac thanked the crowd, praised her opponent and thank her box for their support. At her press conference, Mac was asked by a reporter this question:

"How will you celebrate?"
"… First, I'm going back to WV, sit on my porch and relax. Then I'm going to enjoy a large glass of Earl Grey iced tea with my boyfriend."
"Can you tell us who your boyfriend is?"
"I'm sure you saw him embracing me after the match. He is special and so is my dad."
"Where will you play next?"
"I plan to play the US Open."
"You and Allison McFarland are undefeated this year in doubles and have won three consecutive majors. Will you be playing with her in future events?"
"Ever since I met Allison in Australia, my tennis has consistently improved and she is a big reason why. We will partner at the US Open. She is such a terrific player and my lucky charm. We have so much fun on and off the court and I couldn't have done any of this without her by my side."

Mac and her entourage stayed for the Wimbledon Ball and Mac wowed the attendees, as she and Men's Champion Novak Djokovic danced to Taylor Swift's latest hit. After the long flight back to WV, Mac was relieved to be back home. It had been an exhaustive month of tennis and Mac needed a break. Mac and her entourage were met in Elkins by an enthusiastic throng of autograph seekers and even Allison's coach was drawing some attention.

The months before the US Open passed quickly and Mac, Fred, Allison and her coach were off to New York. The short trip in Mac's jet would take about one hour and all were in a great mood as they flew into New York La Guardia Airport. Under tight security, they took a limo to a 5 million dollar mansion located at 36 Wendover #1. The location was a short distance from Arthur Ashe Stadium and featured 7 bedrooms spanning 6,000 square feet. The home's owner had met Mac at the Boodles Exhibition in London and was so impressed with Mac, that he made his home available to Mac's entourage during the US Open.

When the singles draw was announced, Mac and Allison were shocked to learn they had drawn each other in the first round. It was an unfortunate pairing for a myriad of reasons, and both players had their own reservations. Allison did not want to be the one to ruin Mac's chance at tennis history, but she had her own career to think of. Mac disliked having to play her best friend on tour in a second Major. The media had compared the pairing as the equivalent of the Williams' sisters playing each other in the first round of the US Open.

The night before their scheduled first round meeting, Allison and her coach huddled to prepare strategically for the following day's match. Allison seemed distracted and barely heard the plan for her meeting with Mac. Instead, other thoughts filled her head. Allison knew that she owed Mac more than she could ever repay. Her improvement as a player, her improvement as a person and her rise in the rankings were largely due to the generosity of Mac. Her first-class travel, first-class accommodations and meals were paid for entirely by Mac. These money-saving perks were also given to her coach.

Allison's coach had been the Director of Tennis at a wealthy country club in Dayton, OH, when he uncovered the exceptional talent of a 7-year-old named Allison. Ten years later, John made the decision to resign from his country club position to coach and travel full-time with Allison. John had played D-1 tennis at Ohio State and was an Academic All-American his senior year. He went on to play professionally, attaining a world ranking of 352, but he never qualified for a Slam.

He knew that the friendship Mac and Allison cherished was special and he understood how fortunate they were to be part of Mac's entourage. Not only was his player getting noticed, but because of his association with Mac, he was now recognized as a world-class coach. John and Allison discussed different scenarios for tomorrow's match, including whether Allison should just lose gracefully or try to win. Because Mac and Allison had practiced so many times together, they knew each other's strengths and weaknesses as well as their own. So for Allison to give both a good effort and lose intentionally would be easy. John ultimately entrusted Allison to make the right decision on how she chose to play the match.

A sunny day with no wind greeted Mac and Allison, as they entered a sold-out Arthur Ashe Stadium for their afternoon match. It was perfect tennis weather and the sold-out crowd of 24,000 anticipated a high-quality encounter between these two highly-ranked Americans. Two players, both proud and erect, walked out on the hard court of Ashe Stadium to a generous round of applause. They wore identical white Adidas outfits displaying pleated skirts, a modest tank top and Mac's Signature Nike shoes. They could easily be mistaken for twins; same height, same curvy figure, two pony tails, one blonde and one auburn. They both bounced lightly from side to side as they awaited the coin toss from the umpire. Mac won the toss, elected to serve, and after the traditional 5-minute warm up, the highly-anticipated match began.

The majority of the spectators were behind Mac, but Allison did have some support from the mostly New York fans. The level of play was incredible from start to finish. But in the end, Mac prevailed 6-4 in the third set. There were no bathroom breaks, medical timeouts or stalling of any kind. The three-hour match was played without temper tantrums, racquet smashing, line-call challenges or unsportsmanlike conduct. As the crowd showed their appreciation for a magnificent match, Mac and Allison gave each other a long hug afterward, stood at the net and had a heart-to-heart conversation. There were no tears, only friendship and admiration for each other.

"Mac, I'm so lucky to have you as a friend. "You played like the champion you are."
"I'm sorry we had to play each other. Your play was amazing and I hope we can enjoy the rest of the tournament."
"I know I will. Now, it's your turn to finish writing tennis history."
"I'll do my best, now let's go play some doubles and have some fun."

Mac and Allison continued to breeze through the singles and doubles draw until the quarter-finals of singles, where Mac was paired with the Wimbledon phenom Lucy. Lucy was a grass court specialist, but was adjusting to the US Open hard courts nicely. She had battled through the first four rounds without losing a set and seemed to be improving with every match. The English media had great hopes for this talented Brit and the London bookies had only made Mac a slight favorite. Mac was well aware of the recent success of another Brit who had breezed through the 2021 US Open, Emma Raducanu, and was prepared for a difficult match. Even though Mac had beaten Lucy at Wimbledon, she knew this talented teen could be trouble. Mac started the match fast and by playing some of the best tennis of her career, won 6-3 and 6-3.

On day 11, Fred, Allison and her coach, were joined by Scott Flanagan, Jim Chapman, Evan and Anna in Mac's player's box. Mac's entourage now totaled seven and they were enjoying their stately accommodations at 36 Wendover #1.

Mac's semi-final opponent and the #3 seed was Mac's junior nemesis, Emma. She was now an experienced tour veteran and the second-ranked American behind Mac. Emma had lost to Mac at Wimbledon in three close sets, but was determined to take advantage of her second opportunity. Emma and her coach had plotted specifically for a hoped-for encounter with Mac and this was their chance.

This widely-anticipated semi-final match was played on Arthur Ashe with the roof closed due to unpredictable weather. As the American pair entered the Stadium, the packed crowd applauded vigorously for the top-ranked Americans. Emma and Mac were about the same height, but Emma was the more muscular and about 15 pounds heavier. Both players had aggressive styles, whose talents were well-suited for hard courts. Emma got off to a fast start and won the first set with a barrage of winners from both sides. Mac, with help from the partisan crowd won the second set 7-5, with one break of serve. The third set was a back and forth affair with the superior speed and reflexes of Mac being the deciding factor. The final score was 3-6, 7-5 and 6-4 and after three hours of quality tennis, Mac advanced to the finals. After the match, Mac and her entourage gathered at the player's café, where Mac and Allison nourished themselves on a salmon salad and protein smoothie. Allison and Mac continued their dominance in doubles in front of sell-out crowds.

In the finals, Mac was pitted against an 18-year-old hard-hitting Californian. Sarah was a lanky 6' 1", who possessed a cannon-like serve that was consistently in the 120+ miles per hour (mph) range. She had come through qualifying and had won 8 straight matches to reach the final. The afternoon match was scheduled on Ashe Stadium with the roof open. Because of the presence of 30 mph winds in the area, the tournament officials had considered closing the roof, but weather forecasters had predicted the front would soon pass and bring sunny conditions and calm to the Stadium.

Mac and Sarah were in stark contrast as they made their entrance into Ashe. Mac was dressed in all-white Adidas skirt and tank top, while Sarah was clothed in an all-black Fila dress, complete with a black visor. Sarah had grown up in Oklahoma City and was used to the 30 mph prevailing winds at the Oklahoma City Tennis Center. At 15, she had moved to the Santa Ana River basin, which is known to have the windiest conditions in CA. She was considered an excellent wind player and knew that the wind could be unpredictable, but with the right mindset could be your friend. On the other hand, high winds in the hills of WV were rare and Mac had limited experience playing in the wind.

As the match began, the forecasters were wrong. The winds remained and Mac struggled to find her rhythm. The hard-hitting Californian quickly found her groove and despite some outstanding defensive play from Mac, won the first set 6-3. The crowd wanted to see more tennis and were behind Mac in the second set. As the wind finally calmed down, Mac stormed back and won the second set 6-4. But Sarah was not finished. Behind a big serve and blistering groundstrokes, Sarah charged ahead and was on the verge of winning the third set. When serving at 5-4, and four points away from victory, Sarah hit two crucial double faults to let Mac back in the match. It was the opening that Mac needed. With the crowd's support, Mac won the next three games to secure a hard-earned victory.

Mac was the US Open Champion and the only American woman in the open era to win the Calendar Grand Slam. Mac finished the Grand Slam season with a singles won-lost record of 52-0. The previous day, Mac and Allison had dominated the final to win the Calendar Grand Slam in doubles.

At the awards ceremony, Mac praised her opponent, thanked the crowd and gave special recognition to her box.

"Without the support of the people in my box, this would not have been possible. Thank you, Scott Flanagan, for your friendship and coaching advice. In my opinion, Scott is the best coach anywhere and runs the best Tennis Academy in the world. Thank you Jim Chapman, who believed in me and made it possible for a young girl from WV to pursue her dreams. I want to thank my boyfriend, who supported me during my darkest hour, I love you, Evan. Thank you dad for your love and all the things you do for me that make playing tennis possible. I want to especially thank my dearest friend and doubles partner Allison, who has been such a valuable contributor to our success this year. I see multiple Slams in her future. And finally, I want to thank my sponsors, Adidas, Nike, Wilson, Mercedes and Rolex for standing by me during the darkest period of my life."

At the press conference, a candid, but always humble Mac shocked the tennis world and the media by making this announcement.

"Today will be my last competitive match on tour. I am officially retiring as of today and will no longer play competitive tennis. I intend to focus on my life after tennis."

A surprised reporter then asked.

"And what is after tennis?"
"Marriage and children."
"Do you have any advice for young girls who might want to follow in your footsteps?"
"I would advise them to follow the advice of the legendary poet Maya Angelou, who famously said. *Do the best you can, until you know better, Then when you know better, do better.*"

And with that response, Mac abruptly left the press room to celebrate with friends and family. Fred and Evan stayed a few days longer in New York, while Mac did several photo shoots for her sponsors. She and Allison gave a clinic for underprivileged children in Harlem and Mac was the honored guest at a filet mignon luncheon sponsored by Nike. CEO John Donahoe and founder, Phil Knight were both in attendance and were all smiles as they congratulated Mac on her US Open victory. After an evening of celebration in their borrowed mansion, Mac, Fred, Allison and her coach took the short flight from NY to Elkins and were greeted by a few thousand WV fans seeking selfies and autographs. Mac and Allison patiently tried to satisfy their fans, while Fred and Evan were visibly ignored. When Mac, Fred and Evan were finally back in Valley Head, Mac and Fred responded to numerous calls inquiring about exhibitions, speaker engagements, sponsorships, and personal appearances. Mac's Instagram account had exploded and she stayed busy posting photos and reels of her tennis travels. She was now the most followed female athlete in the world. After a busy week of dealing with admirers, she was worn out physically and mentally.

Relaxing on her porch with Evan at her side, she was finally able to decompress. On this October evening, a full moon pierced the cloudless sky above and the night's sounds danced with the nearby rushing water of the Tygart Valley River. As Mac and Evan melted in their rockers, Mac was finally at peace. Mac dreamed of their new home on the banks of the Elk River, away from the busy traffic of US 219. The popularity of Snowshoe Resort had exploded in recent years and the sounds of 18-wheelers was not to her liking, Mac and Evan were in love and both wanted marriage, but Evan was conflicted. He had prayed about his betrayal regularly and prayed that Mac could forgive him. She had regained the effervescent personality that Evan knew and loved. She was still the kind, humble person that made friends easily. Her charisma remained undeniable. Evan knew he was a lucky man, but did he deserve her love?

Chapter 27

W hile Mac was relaxing and discussing the future with Evan, Fred was busy with exhibition requests and diversifying Mac's wealth. Mac had benefitted greatly by not having to pay for coaches, trainers, psychologists or agents. Fred and Scott had assumed those roles and that had added greatly to Mac's multi-million dollar fortune. Fred estimated Mac's wealth at about $400 million. Her sponsor contracts were worth millions more in the future. Mac was wealthy, healthy and famous. She had been able to play tennis in the present and use her extraordinary talents to end the year undefeated. Had her luck changed?

In late October, Fred called a family meeting with Mac and Evan to discuss Mac's tennis future. He was well-aware that Mac had retired from competitive tennis, but multiple opportunities beckoned and he wanted everyone on the same page. Fred had fielded several lucrative offers for exhibitions and wanted some feedback from Mac. He began the meeting with a question for Mac.

"Sweetheart, I know you've retired from competitive tennis, but how do you feel about doing some exhibitions?"
"I don't think so dad. I played a lot of tennis this year and I am really tired."
"Before you make a final decision, hear me out. There are several organizations around the world that are offering upwards of $5 million for an exhibition and additional amounts for a clinic."
"Dad, I have plenty of money. You can tell them I'm not interested."
"I know you would like to help those in need and I think this could be an opportunity to create a foundation with a global reach."
"How would that work?"
"I believe I could organize a 4-week world tour that would net $40 million dollars and could be used as seed money for a global foundation to help those in need. In addition, the publicity generated would likely attract wealthy donors around the world that would donate money for a worth-while cause."
"Do you think it could make a difference on a global scale?"
"Yes, I think it would."
"Can I call Allison and see it she would go with me? I would need someone to play against."
"Sure, that would be great. Also see if her coach might want to go and help with clinics."

The next day Mac and Allison discussed Fred's plan for a global foundation. Allison seemed interested and told Mac that she would discuss this with her coach. A week later, Allison confirmed their interest, but said that she and her coach wanted some idea as to the financial arrangement. After a consultation with Fred, a rough projection estimated that Allison would be paid one million dollars per exhibition and John $250,000 for each clinic. Since they would have their travel and accommodations paid for, Allison should be able to clear at least $6 million and her coach $1 million. The rest of the money would go to Mac's foundation. The exhibitions would take place in February, which would give organizers time to promote, line up sponsors, distribute TV rights and sell tickets. This framework was based on Fred's communications with numerous countries and organizations around the world. Fred estimated it would take three months to finalize the tour.

The next three months were some of the best times of Mac's life. She had achieved her tennis dream and had the financial resources to help the needy. All that was left was to embark on a future with Evan. It was something Evan wanted, but felt he should wait until after the February exhibition tour.

Both Mac and Evan were heavily involved with church activities. Mac regularly taught Sunday school and Evan developed a user-friendly church website that in addition to the latest church news, developed a church app to make online giving easy and convenient.

With the arrival of February, Fred's plan had taken shape. Mac, Fred, Allison and her coach John had all committed to a 4-week exhibition tour to the following cities. Munich, Germany; Riyadh, Saudi Arabia; Dubai, United Arab Emirates (UAE); Shanghai, China; Beijing, China; Tokyo, Japan. The tour stops would include an exhibition between Mac and

Allison plus an instructional clinic involving Mac, Allison and her coach, John. Fred committed to pay Allison, at least $6 million and John, at least $1 million dollars. Fred calculated the foundation would net roughly $35-40 million. Because of their treatment of women, Saudi Arabia and the UAE were viewed by the media as controversial stops, but Mac and Allison felt that the foundation would offset this argument and be a powerful force for women's rights.

As the tour start neared, Mac and Allison held a joint press conference in Riggleman Hall on the University of Charleston (UC) campus, to address the negativity in the media. After an opening statement by Mac, the first question went to Mac.

"Mac, you've had such success financially and personally in tennis. Are you doing this for the money?"
"Yes and no. Allison and John will be compensated for their time, but I will not be personally compensated. The majority of the funds generated will go to the *MacKenzie Global Foundation*. This is a new Foundation, organized to help the needy around the globe. It will have a special focus on children and improving the lives of women who live in oppressive societies."
"But, aren't you overlooking the plight of women with stops in two Middle East countries?"
"Not at all. We want to showcase our talents as an example of what women are capable of achieving, particularly in sports."

The next questions went to Allison.

"We all know how close you are to Mac and what a great player you are. Do you have any reservations about participating in this exhibition tour?"

"Absolutely none. I think the Foundation will achieve great things and a global tour should attract additional funds from philanthropists worldwide."

"Since Mac has officially retired, are you ready to assume her place atop the world rankings and win your own major titles in singles?"

"Ever since my association with my good friend Mac, I've been able to improve all aspects of my tennis. Concerning major titles in singles, I will give it my best."

After Mac thanked the press, the press conference concluded, and she and Fred returned to Valley Head. They were both pleased with how the event unfolded. Fred told Mac some notable information about how payments would be transferred. Fred had set up an account to handle all revenue from the tour. Organizers would have to wire the money to this account, when Mac and Allison arrived in the destination city. Since Fred didn't completely trust the event planners, Mac and Allison would be paid in advance.

The Valley Head weather in February can be cold and snowy and it was nice to have the indoor court available for practice. Allison had just returned from the AO, where she made the semi-finals in singles. After enduring the commercial flights to and from Australia, she and John greatly missed travelling in Mac's private jet. Before the start of the exhibition tour, Allison decided to rest in Dayton to recover from her travel down under. Mac practiced on her indoor court with her ball machine. Both felt they would experience plenty of practice time during their 6-city tour.

The big day finally arrived and Mac and Fred met Allison and John in Elkins to embark on a 9-hour flight to Munich. After landing in Muenchen Airport, the foursome were taken by limousine to a private residence near the exhibition site. The organizers were the same group that hold the ATP 250 BMW event held yearly at the Munich Club Iphitos. The venue has 17 clay courts and 3 indoor courts. The main stadium only accommodates 4,300 spectators and was sold out during the same week it was announced. After a successful exhibition and clinic in Munich, it was off to Riyadh, Saudi Arabia.

After a 6-hr flight, they landed at King Khaled International Airport and were greeted by Crown Prince Mohammed bin Salman and his entourage. Mac, and her team were given lavish accommodations inside his Al Yamama Palace. The exhibition site was a brand new tennis complex built by and named for the Crown Prince. A crowd of 10,000 spectators watched Mac and Allison give spectators a spectacular show of world-class tennis. It was the largest crowd to attend a tennis event in Saudi Arabia history and the majority in the crowd were women. Rafael Nadal, the new Ambassador of Tennis for Saudi Arabia, presented Mac and Allison diamond tennis bracelets to commemorate the event. A private clinic for the Crown Prince's children was given the following day. The next stop would be Dubai in the UAE.

After a short 1-hr flight to Dubai International Airport, Mac's team was greeted by representatives of ruler Mohammed bin Rashid Al Maktuum and escorted to the iconic Armani Hotel Dubai located in the world's tallest building, the Burj Khalifa. Once settled in their suite, they enjoyed 24-hr butler service plus other amenities. The next day they were chauffeured to the Dubai Duty Free Tennis Stadium, where they were greeted by a sold-out crowd of 5,000. The exhibition was followed by a well-received clinic for children of the royal family.

The next day, Mac joined Allison to play on the world's highest tennis court. Located on a converted helipad on the Burj Al Arab Hotel, it is situated 211 meters above the water. The court offers breath-taking views of the city's skyline and the Arabian Gulf.

Then it was off to Beijing, China. The 7-hr flight to the Beijing Capital International Airport was smooth and allowed for much needed naps by all (except the pilots of course). Mac's team was met by officials of the Chinese Tennis Association, who accompanied them to the Hilton Beijing, which was a 30-minute drive from the Airport. They checked into adjoining King Ambassador Suites, where they prepared for the next day's exhibition by dining on Peking duck. Because of Fred's love of the Hilton, Mac suspected her dad had arranged for their accommodations. The exhibition was held at the China National Tennis Center on the Lotus Court Stadium, with a seating capacity of 10,000. The two tall American ladies entered the Stadium to polite applause and then thoroughly entertained the crowd. A clinic for selected children was held after the exhibition and during a post exhibition press conference, Mac charmed the reporters with her command of Mandarin Chinese. Mac and her team stayed an extra day to visit the Great Wall of China and to see the giant pandas in the Beijing Zoo.

The next stop was Shanghai. The short 1 ½ hour flight to Hongqiao Airport was just minutes from the Qi Zhong Stadium and the Greentown Shanghai Rose Garden Resort. Over 13,000 fans greeted the two tall elegant women, who treated them to a world-class display of power tennis. Mac was able to communicate in Shanghaies with sponsors during a meet and greet after the clinic. Mac and her team also found time to have lunch atop the iconic Oriental Pearl Tower in the Revolving Restaurant and then it was off to Tokyo.

The flight time from Shanghai to Tokyo was just under 3 hours and Mac's team was housed in the Royal Park Hotel Tokyo, which was a 9-minute drive from the exhibition site. The exhibition was played in front of 10,000 fans, with the Ariake Coliseum roof closed due to rainy weather. The rain did not dampen the enthusiasm of the fans, however, as Mac and Allison dazzled the fans with 2 hours of spectacular shot-making.

The 14-hr flight back home to Elkins had finally concluded and Mac's team and the flight crew were exhausted. The 4-week trip had been planned beautifully by Fred, and all parties were paid handsomely for their efforts.

Chapter 28

*E*veryone was more than happy to be home. It had been a successful tour, but grueling, and Mac and Fred were ready for a nice long break. But there was no break for Allison and her coach, as they began preparation for the Indian Well's BNP Paribus Open.

Mac was busy preparing for the next chapter in her life and she was patiently waiting for Evan to ask for her hand in marriage. One day, while leaving church services, Mac asked Evan a probing question.

"Evan, you seemed worried about something. What is it?"
"Oh, it's nothing."
"Evan, I've know you for a long time and I can tell when something is bothering you."

"It's just that I have something I need to tell you and I'm waiting for the right time."

"Evan, you know you can tell me anything, anytime and anywhere."

"I know, but it needs to be special. Why don't we have dinner at Appalachian Kitchen and we can celebrate your tennis success, your Wimbledon title and the success of the tour."

"How about Saturday night."

"Okay, that sounds great."

Evan had reserved the entire restaurant at Appalachian Kitchen for this special evening with Mac. Soft romantic music created the background, as Evan initiated a delicate conversation. He began by looking squarely into Mac's gorgeous blue eyes and said.

"I want to tell you something… I need to…"

"Excuse me for interrupting, Evan. But I want you to know that *I am crazy in love with you.*"

With that, Evan continued, but this time did not look at Mac, but looked down at his plate. He was visibly troubled and was starting to perspire.

"I need to tell you something that's been bothering me…"

Mac sensed something was wrong. Her mind raced as she considered the possibilities. Had he accepted a job at California's Liverpool Lab, to work on fusion reactors? Or maybe working with project Zeus developing high-tech lasers at the University of Michigan (UM)? Or worse yet, does he have a terminal illness? Evan began to sweat as he worked up the courage to tell the love of his life about his transgression.

Just as Evan began to speak, a flash of lightning extinguished the electrical lighting in the restaurant, Moments later, thunder reverberated among the hills of Randolph County, leaving only candles to flicker gently at the table. Mac knew this could not be part of Evan's elaborate plan for the evening, but thought it might be an omen.

A shaken Evan continued...

The End

Mac's Professional Journey

Abbreviations

ACT – American College Testing

AO – Australian Open

AKC – American Kennel Club

ATP – Association of Tennis Professionals (men)

BNP – Banque National de Paris

CPR – Cardiopulmonary Resuscitation

LTA – Lawn Tennis Association (English)

NCAA – National Collegiate Athletic Association

PTSD – Post-Traumatic Stress Disorder

SAT – Scholastic Aptitude Test

SW19 – Wimbledon address

WTA – Women's Tennis Association

UC – University of Charleston

USPTA – United States Professional Tennis Association

USTA – United States Tennis Association

UAE – United Arab Emirates

ZEUS – Zeta-Equivalent Ultrashort pulse Laser System

Printed in Dunstable, United Kingdom